JOSEPH NEEF

To My Daughter
Laura Lee

JOSEPH NEEF
THE AMERICANIZATION OF PESTALOZZIANISM

GERALD LEE GUTEK

The University of Alabama Press
University, *Alabama*

Library of Congress Cataloging in Publication Data

Gutek, Gerald Lee.
  Joseph Neef : the Americanization of Pestalozzianism.

  Bibliography: p.
  Includes index.
  1. Pestalozzi, Johann Heinrich, 1746–1827.
2. Neef, Joseph, 1770–1854. 3. Education—Philosophy. 4. Education—United States—Curricula.
LB628.G76   370.1'092'4   77–1456
ISBN 0–8173–9110–X

CONTENTS

The author wishes to acknowledge
a grant from Loyola University
of Chicago in support of
the publication of this book.

PREFACE

During the research and writing of this book on the educational theory and contributions of Joseph Neef, I have incurred many obligations. I am indebted to the Research Committee of Loyola University of Chicago for a grant that helped me in my initial investigation of the educational ideas of Johann Heinrich Pestalozzi. It was my work with Pestalozzianism that led me to Joseph Neef who was its first promoter in the United States.

A research grant from the American Philosophical Society in 1968 and a summer stipend from the National Foundation for the Humanities in 1970 gave the time and assistance that I needed to use the collections of the Illinois Historical Survey of the University of Illinois and the Workingmen's Institute and Library of New Harmony, Indiana. Dr. Robert Sutton and his associates at the Illinois Historical Survey were most helpful in locating material and in providing an atmosphere that was conducive to research. All who work with the New Harmony collection at the Library of the University of Illinois are indebted to Dr. Arthur Bestor who organized much of the materials.

My visits to New Harmony, Indiana, the scene of much of Neef's life, have always been delightful experiences. I am obligated to Mrs. Aline Cook and to the staff of the Workingmen's Institute and Library for their assistance in facilitating my research.

I appreciate the kindness of Matthew Creighton, S.J., of the Classics Department of Loyola University, who translated Neef's frequent Latin and Greek phrases. Father Creighton's comments on Neef's ideas on the value of the classics and on foreign language instruction were most helpful.

I am grateful to my colleagues and students in the Foundations of Education Department of Loyola University for encouraging my investigation of the American phases of the Pestalozzian movement. Appreciation is due to the members of the Midwest History of Education Society for their interest in my work on Neef.

My interest in Neef and in the educators of New Harmony has been a continuing one. I thank my wife, Patricia, for sharing it with me.

Chicago, Illinois   Gerald Lee Gutek

PART ONE

The Life of Joseph Neef

1

JOSEPH NEEF'S EARLY CAREER

At the south edge of New Harmony, Indiana, in Maple Hill cemetery, over the grave of Joseph Neef, there is a monument erected by his daughter, Mrs. Richard Owen, which bears the inscription, "Joseph Neef was a coadjutor of Pestalozzi, in Switzerland and was the first to promulgate the Pestalozzian system of education in America." Educational historians have mirrored the epitaph on Neef's stone memorial and have interpreted him as the lengthened shadow of Johann Heinrich Pestalozzi in America.[1] Although he was a reflection of his Swiss mentor, Neef was also an educational theorist in his own right. While Pestalozzi was a European who tried to introduce his system of natural education through paternalistic means, Neef quickly accepted the frontier egalitarianism of his adopted nation. This book will examine and analyze Neef's philosophy of education which blended both Pestalozzian and republican principles.

Joseph Neef has been recognized by educational historians as one of the first persons to introduce the Pestalozzian method of education into the United States. As a friend and associate of William Maclure, pioneer American geologist and philanthropic patron of science and education, Neef came to the United States in 1806 and subsequently established Pestalozzian schools in Pennsylvania, Kentucky, Indiana, and Ohio. His *A Sketch of a Plan and Method of Education*, published in 1808, which acquainted Americans with Pestalozzian education, has been frequently cited as the first pedagogical book to be written in English in the United States. Neef also participated in Robert Owen's famous communitarian social experiment at New Harmony, Indiana. Although he is mentioned in most of the standard works on American educational history, Neef's theory of education has been treated only superficially. This examination of Neef's life and educational theory will describe: one, his encounter with and acceptance of Pestalozzi's educational method; two, his association with William Maclure and his introduction of Pestalozzianism into the United States; three, his participation in the Owenite social experiment at New Harmony; four, his career as an educational reformer; five, his development of an educational philosophy and curriculum based on sense realism, rationalism, republicanism, and Pestalozzianism.

Early Life   Francis Joseph Nicholas Neef was born in the Alsatian town of Soultz, on December 6, 1770, to Francis Joseph Neef, the local miller, and his wife, the former Anastasia Ackerman. Although of German origin, the Neefs were loyal Frenchmen. Young Joseph, who was to be a Pestalozzian teacher of languages, learned both French and German which were spoken in the bilingual provinces of Alsace-Lorraine. As the son of a middle-class family, Neef enjoyed the educational privileges of his class. At his father's urging, Joseph began studies for the Roman Catholic priesthood in the school conducted by the monks of the Abbey of Murbach. Here, he revealed his propensity for foreign languages by quickly learning Latin, Greek, and Italian.

Along with many other young men of the late eighteenth century, Neef's education was interrupted by the advent of the French Revolution. Inspired by the revolutionary slogans of "Liberty, Equality, and Fraternity," he became an ardent advocate of the "Rights of Man." As a convinced republican and a patriotic Frenchman, twenty-one year old Neef left the monastery school in 1791 to join the armies of France. Throughout his life, Neef maintained his republican zeal and belief in the essential equality of all men.

In the French Army, Neef served as a noncommissioned, adjutant subofficer in the Second Brigade, Fifth Division of the

Army of the Rhine. During the time of his service, the French Army was organized into light demibrigades of from 1,000 to 1,500 men and demibrigades of battle, composed of 3,000 men. Four of these demibrigades comprised an infantry division.[2] Neef became familiar with Napoleon's tactical strategy of employing highly mobile infantry formations which moved rapidly under the close coordination of concentrated artillery fire. He saw combat in the Italian campaign, in which the outnumbered French forces faced the immobile, cumbersome, but larger Austrian army. Burton, an historian of the Italian campaign, provides the following account of the *élan* of the French army:

> The French soldiery, inspired by the enthusiasm of the new republican era, were splendid, and almost invincible as long as they believed themselves to be so. The infantry was the best in Europe and contained the finest elements in the army.[3]

In 1796, the Austrians mounted a desperate counteroffensive to push Napoleon's army out of Italy. Neef was among the defenders of Arcole, where the beleaguered French stemmed the Austrian advance. The battle of Arcole was a crucial French victory and was also a major crisis in Neef's life. He was seriously wounded by an Austrian round which entered his head between the right eye and the nose; it remained there until after his death.[4] This battle wound caused severe physical pain throughout Neef's life as the occasionally shifting position of the round caused headaches and fainting spells. Owing to the severity of the wound, Neef was discharged from the army and awarded an honorable certificate of service by the administrative council of the Second Brigade which attested that he had:

> . . . comported himself courageously, honorably, and honestly, that his conduct and his deportment have never ceased to be worthy of a true Republican, and that he had distinguished himself as much by his zeal for the service as by his military knowledge.[5]

While recuperating in a military hospital, Neef read the works of the Swiss educator Johann Heinrich Pestalozzi, 1746–1827, who had published *The Evening Hour of a Hermit* in 1780, and

Leonard and Gertrude in 1781. Of the two books, *Leonard and Gertrude* enjoyed a greater public popularity as a romantic novel depicting the struggle of simple Swiss peasants to achieve social regeneration through a program of natural education.[6] However, the more philosophical work, *The Evening Hour of a Hermit*, impressed the ailing soldier. Seeking to create meaning in his own life, Neef identified with Pestalozzi's philosophical quest to discover the means by which each man might achieve personal peace and perfection.[7] It was not surprising that the wounded Neef's search for a new vocation ended with his decision to become a school teacher.

With Pestalozzi at Burgdorf   Neef, who regarded himself as a loyal disciple of Pestalozzi, has been interpreted by educational historians as the earliest practitioner of Pestalozzian pedagogy in the United States. In that light, an examination of Neef's educational experience with Pestalozzi is necessary to determine some of the influences of the Swiss educator. Neef's first personal encounter with Pestalozzi occurred at the educational institute of Burgdorf, which the latter had founded in 1800. Although it closed in 1804, the four years of the Burgdorf institute's existence were significant for both Pestalozzi and Neef.

Pestalozzi had conducted shortlived schools at Neuhof, 1774–1779, and at Stans, 1799, but it was at Burgdorf that he worked out the major procedures of his method of natural education. The more abstract and theoretical aspects of the method were devised at his last and most famous institute at Yverdon, 1805–1825. At Burgdorf, Pestalozzi was more concerned with developing a concrete method of education. At Yverdon, German Idealism entered into Pestalozzi's formulation of an educational philosophy and obscured certain aspects of his method of instruction. Neef escaped much of the obscurantism which characterized Pestalozzi's later work at Yverdon. The years at Burgdorf were an important apprenticeship for Neef who directly witnessed the development of the methodological phase of Pestalozzianism and who had the opportunity to practice the method under the tutelage of the system's originator. Before commenting more fully on Neef's apprenticeship, some mention is needed of Pestalozzi's reasons for establishing the institute at Burgdorf.

Upon arriving at Burgdorf, Pestalozzi was regarded as a visionary eccentric by most of the townspeople. His reputation as an inefficient and muddleheaded administrator had preceded him. He was not permitted to conduct his own school but rather assigned to the elementary school for working-class children which was conducted by Samuel Dysli, the village shoemaker. Dysli regarded Pestalozzi as a rival and would not cooperate with the newcomer. Distrusting Pestalozzi's unconventional teaching methods, Dysli intrigued against him and eventually secured his rival's dismissal.

Dysli's elementary school illustrated the traditional manner of school teaching which Pestalozzi vehemently rejected and which Neef came to oppose. Considered a menial rather than a professional undertaking, elementary school teaching had degenerated into school keeping carried on by individuals like Dysli as a side line rather than a full-time vocation. Usually ignorant of both subject matter and teaching methods, these ill-prepared school keepers taught catechism by rote and supervised the class while individual students pursued their solitary lessons. Dysli insisted, as did the working-class parents, that the children's learning be restricted to memorizing the psalms and the Heidelberg *Catechism*. Pestalozzi's ignoring the catechism and psalter furnished the pretext for his dismissal from Dysli's school.[8] Although Pestalozzi sought to devote his life to educating the poor, his strongest opposition came from that class. He enjoyed his greatest success with middle-class children. Although Neef, too, was interested in educating working-class children, his students came primarily from the middle class.

After his dismissal from Dysli's school, Pestalozzi received a position in a preparatory school in Burgdorf which was attended by middle-class children, ages five to eight. This school conducted by a Madame Stahli provided reading and writing lessons for children who were expected to attend secondary school. Given more freedom to use his own educational method, Pestalozzi began to organize instruction into what he considered to be the simplest, first elements. In recounting this experience, he later wrote:

I sought in every way to simplify the elements of reading and counting and to reduce them to a psychological connection; so that the child could pass easily from the first step to the second, from the second to the third, &c.[9]

The reduction of learning into simplified and graduated exercises was a major aspect of Pestalozzi's method. These learning exercises were to be appropriate to the child's stage of readiness. A major premise was that learning should not be hurried but rather was to be slow, thorough, and complete. Pestalozzi's method was so successful at Madame Stahli's schools that he began to win praise in Burgdorf. On March 31, 1800, the Burgdorf School Commission examined his teaching method and issued a favorable report:

Whilst by the laborious method hitherto pursued children from five to eight years of age only learn the letters, to spell and read, your pupils have not only accomplished this task with such a degree of perfection as we have not met with before, but the cleverest among them distinguished themselves by their beautiful writing, their talent for drawing and counting. You have succeeded with all in arousing and cultivating the taste for history, natural history, measuring, geography, &c. in such a way that their future masters will see their work incredibly simplified if they are able to take advantage of this preparation.[10]

Under the favorable auspices of the Commission's "Report," the Helvetian government granted Pestalozzi the rent-free use of Burgdorf castle as an educational institute for the instruction of children and the preparation of teachers. It also agreed to pay Pestalozzi a salary as director of the institution, to subsidize a number of teaching assistants who were to be trained as teachers, and to aid in the publication of textbooks. With this financial support, Pestalozzi's institution opened in January, 1801 and functioned for three and a half years until the government reclaimed the old castle in June 1804.

Neef's Apprenticeship at Burgdorf   As indicated, Pestalozzi's books had stimulated Neef's interest in education and had convinced him to become a teacher. When the news of the opening of the institute at Burgdorf reached him, Neef arranged an interview with Pestalozzi to seek a position as a member of the faculty. In addition to his proficiency in French, German, and classical languages, Neef's career as a soldier had left him with a special interest in gymnastics, military tactics, and drill. Since he possessed these skills and seemed to be dedicated to education, Pestalozzi welcomed him to the faculty of the institute. Pestalozzi appointed him instructor of foreign languages and gymnastics. He believed that Neef would become a competent teacher with preparation in the special method of natural education. From this time on, a close personal and professional relationship developed and grew between the two men. When Neef reflected on his decision to become a teacher, he later wrote, he decided to cultivate the "bewildered field of education" in order to benefit his fellow citizens. Although some regarded teaching as a "painful occupation," Neef believed that his "habits of thinking," "temper," and "experience" qualified him for the vocation.[11]

As one of over twenty teaching assistants, Neef joined the circle of fellow instructors who comprised the household of the Burgdorf institute. Wanting to preside over the institute as a father figure, the paternalistic Pestalozzi sought to cultivate a secure family relationship in the school. Since he insisted that all instruction was to occur within a climate of emotional love and security, Pestalozzi's program of teacher preparation required more than the mastery of methodological skills. It also involved a close personal relationship between the master teacher and the apprentices by which those who sought to emulate the master would eventually become his disciples. Joseph Neef, as well as many of the others trained at Burgdorf, became loyal Pestalozzian disciples who later carried the method of natural education throughout Europe and America. Neef, the first Pestalozzian educator in the United States, left Burgdorf as a convinced and skilled practitioner of the natural method of education. While each of the teachers trained by Pestalozzi could rightfully claim to be his heir, each one gave a unique interpretation to his method of education. When Neef established his schools in the United States and wrote his pedagogical treatises, he, to, developed his own distinctive version of Pestalozzianism. His concept of natural education was grounded on rationalistic principles rather than on the emotional paternalism which Pestalozzi had employed.

As a member of the Burgdorf faculty from 1800 to 1803, Neef became acquainted with a number of teaching assistants who later achieved distinction as Pestalozzian educators. Such individuals as Hermann Krusi, J. G. Tobler, Johannes Buss, Johannes Niederer, and Johannes Ramsauer, as well as Neef, were to contribute to the diffusion of Pestalozzian pedagogy. Although precise influences cannot be traced, it is not unwarranted to believe that these young educators were stimulated by their mutual association with Pestalozzi and with each other.

Neef's Associates at Burgdorf   At the Burgdorf institute, Neef associated with Hermann Krusi, 1775–1844, one of Pestalozzi's first assistants, and the man who had brought a number of poor children from the war-devastated region of Appenzell to be received by "Papa Pestalozzi." Described as "intelligent but unassuming, willing to learn, and warm-hearted," Krusi worked with Pestalozzi for almost twenty years.[12] His son, Hermann Krusi, Jr., was associated with Edward A. Sheldon at the Oswego Normal School in New York during a revival of Pestalozzianism in the United States in the latter half of the nineteenth century.

J. G. Tobler, 1769–1843, also from Appenzell, was a friend of Krusi. In order to earn enough money to begin theological study at Basle, he had worked as a manual laborer and then decided to become a teacher. After Tobler joined the institute at Burgdorf, he persuaded Pestalozzi to accept his friend, Johannes Buss, 1776–1855, as the teacher of art, drawing, and mathematics. The son of a minor official in the theological school at Tübingen, Buss had received a classical education and was an able student of Greek, Hebrew, logic, rhetoric, drawing, and music. Despite Buss' academic versatility, his lower-class origins precluded further education in Germany. In financial difficulties, he left school, took up bookbinding, and wandered into Switzerland. Hearing of Pestalozzi's work, Buss ventured to Burgdorf where, upon Tobler's recommendation, he was accepted as a teacher. Although he had been warned against having any connection with the eccentric Swiss educator, Buss quickly became a disciple of Pestalozzi. The following account records Buss's first impression of Pestalozzi:

At our first interview, he came down from an upper room with his stockings about his heels, and his coat covered with dust. His whole appearance was so miserable that I was inclined to pity him; yet there was something in his expression so grand that I looked upon him with veneration. His benevolence, the cordial reception he gave me, his unpretending simplicity, and the dilapidated condition in which he stood before me—the whole man impressed me powerfully. I was his in one instant. No man had ever so sought my heart, none so won my confidence.[13]

Like Buss, Neef was also attracted to the visionary Swiss educator who had been branded by his opponents as a dismal failure, an eccentric, and even as a lunatic destined for an insane asylum. Pestalozzi's obsession with developing a natural method of education and of regenerating the poor caused a single-minded dedication to his work and neglect of personal appearance and ambition. Neef was inspired by his association with Pestalozzi whom he later described as being characterized by "goodness of his heart" and the "soundness of his head."[14]

Also among Pestalozzi's assistants was Johannes Niederer, 1779–1843, who because of his training in divinity and theology was the Protestant chaplain and teacher of Scripture. Niederer was well-versed in the German philosophic Idealism of Fichte and Schelling and as Pestalozzi's secretary introduced some of their abstract metaphysical concepts into his writing.[15]

During Neef's apprenticeship at Burgdorf, Pestalozzi was concerned with concrete educational practices rather than with attempts to construct a systematic educational philosophy. Since Neef's association with Pestalozzi occurred during the more practical and methodological stage of development of natural education, Neef could claim that Pestalozzian pedagogy was immediately useful and uncluttered by transcendental concepts. However, by 1812, Maclure was writing to Neef about the "rather dark subjects" of religion and morals which were being discussed at Yverdon. Maclure believed that it was difficult to reconcile such transcendental subjects with the basic principles of the method.[16]

Johannes Ramsauer, who was a student at Burgdorf when Neef was teaching languages and gymnastics, later wrote a detailed description of Pestalozzi's educational practices, and revealed the affection which the students at Burgdorf castle had for Neef. Later, Neef's American students would have the same respect and affection for the man who they invariably described as an "old soldier." It is interesting that Ramsauer should have referred to Neef as an "old soldier" with a "crabbed face," since at this time he was only thirty-one or thirty-two years old. According to Ramsauer's description:

This Neef was an old soldier who had fought in all parts of the world. He was a giant with a great beard, a crabbed face, a severe air, and rude exterior, but he was kindness itself. When he marched with the air of a trooper at the head of sixty or eighty children, his great voice thundering a Swiss air, then he enchanted the whole house. I should say that Neef, in spite of the rudeness of his exterior was the pupil's favourite, and for this reason that he lived always with them, and felt happiest when amongst them. He played, exercised, walked, bathed, climbed, threw stones, with the scholars all in a childish spirit; this is how he had such unlimited authority over them. Meanwhile he was not a pedagogue, he only had the heart of one.[17]

Among the students at Burgdorf, there was a girl who would become the wife of Joseph Neef. Eloisa Buss, 1784–1846, the only girl enrolled in the school, was the sister of Johannes Buss, who had persuaded Pestalozzi to admit her as a student. She became a member of the large household and was placed in the special care of Madame Pestalozzi. Neef was Eloisa's French tutor and a mutual attraction arose between the couple. In 1803, Pestalozzi sent Neef to Paris to establish a school modeled on his educational method. Before he left Burgdorf, Joseph Neef and Eloisa Buss were betrothed. On July 5, 1803, the two were married by proxy in a ceremony performed in Burgdorf castle and witnessed by Pestalozzi and his wife.[18] At the time of their wedding, Neef was thirty-three years old and his wife was nineteen. During the forty-three years of their marriage, a strong bond of love united them. Eloisa was educated in the Pestalozzian method and assisted Neef in his schools in the United States. Since she was very capable, her husband relied on her to administer the practical and financial affairs of their family and of the schools which they conducted.

Pestalozzian Methodology at Burgdorf The Pestalozzian institute at Burgdorf was the seedbed of the pedagogical principles which Neef would import to the United States and which others would diffuse throughout Europe. In 1800, Pestalozzi wrote *The Method, A Report by Pestalozzi* for the Society of the Friends of Education, an organization formed to advance, support, and popularize his work. The *Report*, which represented Pestalozzi's first attempt to describe his method systematically, began with the words, "I am trying to psychologize the instruction of mankind." He indicated that he wanted to organize instruction according to the laws of human nature and development. In conformity to nature, he sought to simplify the elements of human knowledge by reducing them into a graduated series of instruction. According to his *Report*:

I have tried to simplify the elements of all human knowledge according to these laws, and to put them into a series of typical examples that shall result in spreading a wide knowledge of Nature, general clearness of the most important ideas in the mind, and vigorous exercises of the chief bodily powers, even among the lowest classes.[19]

A brief examination of Pestalozzi's pedagogical principles as stated in the *Report* aid in establishing the educational context at Burgdorf and provide an idea of the instructional method which Neef learned while a member of the institute's faculty. Pestalozzi emphasized that sense impression was the "only true foundation of human instruction" because it was the "only true foundation of human knowledge."[20] Throughout his educational career, Neef followed the Pestalozzian stress on sensation and used it as the basis for the object lessons which he devised. In developing an instructional methodology based on sense experience, Pestalozzi followed the advice which he gave to others in his *Report*:

In every subject try to arrange graduated steps of knowledge, in which every new idea shall be only a small, almost imperceptible addition to that earlier knowledge which has been deeply impressed and made unforgettable.

Learn to make the simple perfect before going on to the complex.[21]

When Neef wrote his own *Sketch of a Plan and Method of Education*, he adhered closely to these basic methodological principles. He agreed that instruction should be unhurried, gradual, and complete. Further, Neef affirmed that all learning was the result of sensation.

In addition to stressing sensation, Pestalozzi's emphasis on the creation of an environment of love and emotional security, rather than of repression and coercion, was a major departure from traditional schooling. Permissive teacher-student relationships were carefully cultivated at Burgdorf to foster this climate of security. At least two teachers were with the students to share in their meals and games. This close association between teacher and learner rested on Pestalozzi's premise that learning proceeded most efficiently in an emotionally secure environment from which fear of punishment, pain, and ridicule was banished.

When he established his own schools in the United States, Neef also cultivated permissive classroom relationships but a difference developed between the educational permissiveness of Pestalozzi and Neef. According to his highly emotional view of child nature and romanticized concept of the role of love in stimulating human growth, Pestalozzi cultivated the image of the kindly father who was paternalistic as well as permissive. Although Neef was also permissive, he regarded himself as a fellow learner along with his students rather than as a father figure. Unlike the romantic and emotional Pestalozzi, Neef was a cool rationalist who believed that freedom from fear and coercion allowed the students a greater freedom in which to develop intellectually and morally.

Once the permissive climate had been created, the students proceeded to Pestalozzi's "special method" known as the "ABC of *Anschauung.*" For Pestalozzi, *Anschauung* referred to the entire process of conceptualization and "ABC" to the process by which instruction was organized on a graduated scale from the simplest components to the complex.

I sought in all ways to bring the beginnings of spelling and counting to the greatest simplicty and into form. So that the child with the greatest psychological order might pass from the first step gradually to the second; and then without break, upon the foundation of the perfectly understood second step, might go on quickly and safely to the third and fourth. But instead of the letters that I made the children draw with their slate pencil, I now led them to draw angles, squares, lines, and curves.[22]

Rather than using the traditional individual recitation, Pestalozzi used simultaneous group instruction, which he believed contributed to socialization and was also more efficient in terms of time than the older method. The students at Burgdorf practiced spelling and reading with the help of movable letters and learned to count with concrete objects such as pebbles and beans. They learned division by cutting up and dividing apples and cakes. Numbers were introduced only after the arithmetical processes were completely understood. Ample opportunities were provided for gymnastic and physical education. The children studied natural science first hand by excursions and field trips into the surrounding countryside. Pestalozzi used real, concrete objects in his lessons wherever possible because he wanted to avoid the highly verbal and abstract lessons which characterized traditional schooling.

Neef thoroughly mastered the Pestalozzian method of instruction, and he based his teaching on it when he came to the United States. His major pedagogical treatise, *The Sketch of a Plan and Method of Education,* was a thoroughly Pestalozzian document. Neef, as well as his colleagues, benefited by their exposure to Pestalozzi and his method of natural education. During the short years of its existence, the Burgdorf institute served as a center for the preparation of Pestalozzian teachers and for the development of learning materials. In 1804, the canton of Berne repossessed Burgdorf castle and Pestalozzi was forced to move his Institute to Yverdon where it remained until 1825.

Neef's School in Paris Two years before Pestalozzi was forced to move, he went to Paris as a member of the Helvetian delegation which sought to negotiate a political settlement for Switzerland with the Napoleonic government. At first, Pestalozzi was enthusiastic about his diplomatic assignment. He hoped to discuss his natural method of education with the French Emperor and perhaps win Napoleon's endorsement for its use in France. Napoleon was too preoccupied with his empire, however, to listen to the eccentric Swiss pedagogue. While in Paris, Pestalozzi was approached by a philanthropic society which requested him to establish an orphan school in Paris according to the plan used at Burgdorf. Pestalozzi, who was disappointed with his Parisian visit and anxious to return to Switzerland, promised that he would send Joseph Neef to Paris to establish the school. Pestalozzi believed that Neef was the logical choice for such a task since he was familiar with France and spoke French fluently.[23] Pestalozzi also felt that Neef had mastered the essentials of the method and could be relied upon to initiate the orphan school in Paris.

At Pestalozzi's recommendation, Neef went to Paris in 1802 and established the orphan school. Although little information is available about this school, Neef apparently was given charge of a number of orphan children and proceeded to educate them according to the Pestalozzian method of natural education. Less than enthusiastic about his situation, Neef forwarded some of his complaints to Pestalozzi. He complained that the French did not really understand Pestalozzi's educational princples, and that some of the materials which described Pestalozzi's theory had been erroneously translated from German into French. Neef also wrote that the children who were sent to his school were handicapped and weak. Although he complained that he was underpaid, unappreciated, and lonely in Paris, Neef expressed his commitment that Pestalozzianism was the "method of intelligence and Nature."[24] Later in the year, Neef's wife Eloisa joined him in Paris, and began to manage many of the routine and practical affairs which her husband typically neglected.

Despite Neef's complaints about his Parisian assignment, the school prospered and attracted a number of visitors who were interested in Pestalozzianism. In 1804, Neef's school was visited by Napoleon, Talleyrand, and other government officials. The visit of the Emperor also brought the American philanthropist, William Maclure, to Neef's school. Maclure had earlier become interested in Pestalozzian education and unsuccessfully attempted to persuade Pestalozzi himself to come to the United States to found a school in Philadelphia. Maclure used his visit to the school to examine Neef's implementation of Pestalozzi's method. He was so impressed that he began negotiations to bring Neef to the United States to introduce the method of natural education and to establish Pestalozzian schools.

2

NEEF'S INTRODUCTION OF PESTALOZZIANISM TO THE UNITED STATES

The meeting of Joseph Neef and William Maclure in Paris in 1804 was an event which held great significance for both men. Maclure came to exert an influence over Neef's life which was not unlike that of Pestalozzi. It was Maclure who persuaded Neef to emigrate to the United States, to establish Pestalozzian schools, and to participate in the Owenite communitarian experiment at New Harmony. Although both Neef and Maclure were committed to and sought to diffuse Pestalozzian education, each of them also added his own ideas to the method. Neef, a firm rationalist, saw the method as an instrument which would liberate and advance man's intelligence. Conceiving of education in sociological terms, Maclure believed that Pestalozzianism would advance the enlightenment, interests, and power of the working class. Through their combined efforts, Pestalozzian educational practice entered the American environment.

William Maclure   William Maclure, 1763–1840, is still an enigma to American social, intellectual, and educational historians. Although some of his strong convictions on politics, economics, society, and education are known, his personal life remains a mystery. His biography still remains unwritten. Little is known of his childhood and youth with the exception that he was born in Ayr, Scotland, on March 22, 1763, the son of a merchant. He received a conventional classical education which he later observed had launched him "into the world as ignorant as a pig of anything useful, not having occasion to practice anything that I had learned."[1] Even before encountering Pestalozzi and Neef, Maclure had criticized traditional education:

I had been long in the habit of considering education one of the greatest abuses our species were guilty of, and of course one of the reforms the most beneficial to humanity, and likewise offering to ambition a fair field. Almost no improvement has been made in it for two or three hundred years; there was immense room for change to put it on a par with other functions of civilization.[2]

Maclure, who made a fortune in commerce, first visited the United States in 1782 and was highly impressed by the young republic. Upon returning to England, he became a partner in the prosperous firm of Miller, Hart, and Company. During the next fifteen years, Maclure traveled extensively supervising the firm's interests. After spending some time in Ireland and France, he came again to the United States in 1796, took up residency, and became a citizen in 1803. He was appointed to the United States Commission in 1803 which went to France to settle claims lodged by American citizens against the French government for property losses suffered during the French Revolution. While on the continent, Maclure traveled widely to collect specimens for a natural history museum and studied the European educational systems.[3]

Although neglected by educational historians, Maclure was an early student of comparative education. In Europe, he visited schools in Germany, Switzerland, and France and met both Emmanuel Fellenberg and Johann Heinrich Pestalozzi. While he was impressed by the efficient operations of Fellenberg's school at Hofwyl, Maclure found the cooperative spirit of Pestalozzi's school at Yverdon more to his liking.[4] Maclure agreed with Pestalozzi that education served social, economic, and political, as well as pedagogical ends. Finding ignorance to be the chief cause of social evil and poverty, both Maclure and Pestalozzi held that societal reform could be achieved only by gradual educational means. Maclure found Pestalozzianism to be the most effective method for diffusing useful knowledge and felt that the open American environment would be conducive to the success of the system of natural education.[5] Maclure commented upon his commitment to Pestalozzianism:

... I have considered ignorance as the cause of all the miseries and errors of mankind and have used all my endeavors to reduce the quantity of that truly diabolical evil. My experience soon convinced me that it was impossible to give any real information to men and that the only possible means of giving useful knowledge to the world was by the education of children. About 15 years ago I stumbled upon the Pestalozzian system, which appeared to me to be the best that I had seen for the diffusion of useful knowledge. I have therefore endeavored to introduce it into the United States of America as the place I thought the most likely to succeed.[6]

Since he was already antagonistic to traditional education, Maclure's encounter with Pestalozzi at Yverdon in 1804 stimulated him to encourage and subsidize the emigration of Pestalozzian educators to the United States. Maclure offered to support Pestalozzi if he agreed to establish an institution in Philadelphia like that of Yverdon. Because of his age and ignorance of English, Pestalozzi declined the offer and instead recommended Joseph Neef, his former assistant.[7] Maclure was so impressed with Neef's teaching that he urged him to emigrate to the United States and establish a Pestalozzian school in Philadelphia. Neef was weary of the deteriorating European situation, and disenchanted with Napoleonic despotism. Since he did not particularly enjoy his work in Paris, Neef eagerly accepted Maclure's invitation and later wrote of his decision:

My soul was warmed with admiration at such uncommon generosity. Republican by inclination and principle, and of course not at all pleased with the new order of things that was established under my eyes, I was not only glad to quit Europe, but I burnt with desire to see that country, to live in, and to be useful to it.[8]

Like Pestalozzi, Neef was apprehensive about his ignorance of English. Maclure quieted Neef's fears by agreeing to guarantee him a sufficient income during the time required to learn the language. Neef agreed to come to the United States and to promulgate the educational system in which both he and Maclure had such great expectations. The two parties agreed to the following contract:

Professor Neef agrees to go to Pennsylvania in the United States of America and to teach children after the methods of Pestalozzi for three years from the date of his arrival, in consequence of which Wm. Maclure agrees to pay Professor Neef's expenses from Paris to the U.S. of America to the amount of three thousand two hundred Livres Tournois and to make good to Professor Neef whatever sum as salary he may receive for teaching same methods that falls short of Five Hundred Dollars per Annum during the three years of time Professor Neef may continue to teach the system of Pestalozzi. Paris, 19th March, 1806.[9]

Neef immediately made plans to bring his family to the United States. On March 20, 1806, J. Cox Barnet, the United States Commerical Agent, issued a certificate which recommended the Neef family to the protection of American officers and citizens while they traveled to America. This certificate specified that Neef had agreed to establish a school in Pennsylvania for the purpose of teaching children according to the Pestalozzian method.[10] Upon arriving in the United States, Neef devoted himself to learning English and to planning for the establishment of his school. During this time, he was subsidized by Maclure according to the provisions of their contract.

Neef's Educational Writing   Before opening his first American school at the Falls of the Schuylkill, near Philadelphia, Neef wrote and in 1808 privately published his *Sketch of a Plan and Method of Education, Founded on an Analysis of the Human Faculties, and Natural Reason, Suitable for the Offspring of a Free People, and for all Rational Beings*. The book's title reveals its author's commitment to rational education and to the cultivation of republican principles. Neef wrote the *Sketch* to familiarize Americans with Pestalozzian pedagogy and to furnish prospective clients of his school with a prospectus of the curriculum and method to be used in educating their children.

Monroe has commented that while Christopher Dock's *Schul-Ordnung* was the oldest American book on educational method, Neef's *Sketch* was the first such work to be written in English in the United States.[11] Many American educational historians have commented on Neef's *Sketch*, among them H. G. Good, who wrote:

The book by Neef is a first-hand account of the Pestalozzian program and the first such account given to Americans. He proposed to have his pupils learn by inquiry and investigation. They would learn old things in a new way. Arithmetic was taught in very short steps, using objects and by having the pupils work out the number combinations. Drawing was to come before writing, and a great deal of oral work before reading. Books were not to be used until after the pupil had made much progress through conversation. In geography the pupils were to measure gardens and fields and draw plans to scale. The book shows Pestalozzi's work in his earlier rather than his Yverdon period.[12]

Certain aspects of the *Sketch* had a direct bearing on the school which Neef established at the Falls of the Schuylkill. He indicated his intention of locating the school near, but not in, a city, and of limiting the enrollment to children of ages six to eight. Since he planned to use simultaneous instruction rather than the older and more time-consuming individual recitation, he wanted a homogeneous group of students. At first, the school day would be limited to four hours of instruction and then gradually lengthened as the student's interest span increased. In order to take advantage of the healthy natural environment, lessons would be conducted out-of-doors as often as possible.[13]

In 1809, Neef translated and published the *Logic of Condillac* as a further illustration of the plan of education used at his school.[14] It is noteworthy that he chose to translate *Condillac,* an empiricist sensationalist philosopher of the eighteenth century Enlightenment, rather than one of Pestalozzi's works. Neef incorporated much of Condillac's epistemology into his own method of object teaching.

In 1813, Neef wrote *The Method of Instructing Children Rationally in the Arts of Writing and Reading.*[15] While certain short passages of this book provide an interesting commentary on the use of sensation as the basis for instruction, most of the *Method* was merely a manual of exercises for use in teaching reading and writing.

The School at the Falls of the Schuylkill   In 1809, Neef opened his school for boys five miles from Philadelphia. Located on a hill a half mile from the Falls of Schuylkill, Neef's establishment consisted of three buildings: the school, the family residence, and a student dormitory. The buildings were "plainly constructed, of rough, substantial materials—but dry, sound, well ventilated—in a primitive way comfortable."[16] Neef's wife, Eloisa, took charge of the domestic arrangements and financial management of the school.

A catalogue of Neef's students at the school indicates that seventy-five students attended. Although the majority were Philadelphians, students also came from Boston, and Northampton, Masachusetts; Louisville, Kentucky; and Savannah, Georgia. Since Neef's students came from various sections of the United States, the existence of the school must have been known in certain circles. Neef's record of his students also includes a description of the vocations and professions which they later pursued as adults. Eight became lawyers, ten merchants, two engineers, and one each became a sea captain, farmer, planter, dentist, traveller, druggist, blacksmith, doctor, coachmaker, minister, and carpenter.[17]

A very illuminating description of student life and study in Neef's school at the Falls appeared in 1867 as an article entitled "Pestalozzi in America," which was based on the reminiscences of one of the Gardette brothers who had attended the school:

I lived at the school for four years (from my seventh to my eleventh year). During this period, I saw no schoolbook, neither was I taught my alphabet. The chief subjects, taught us orally, were the languages, mathematics, and the natural sciences, and the idea was to make us understand the object and application of all we learned.[18]

Gardette's account gave further evidence that Neef's school practices were consistent with the antiverbalism which he shared with his naturalistic predecessors, Rousseau and Pestalozzi. Neef opposed an education which was limited to memorizing bodies of literature, especially the Greek and Latin classics. He believed that the classicalists had ignored sensation and overemphasized literary materials. Since he believed that many students in conventional schools learned to read without really understanding the meaning of the literature, Neef deferred reading instruction until the students' tenth or eleventh year. Before they learned to read, Neef wanted his students to have a broad range of direct experiences which would aid them in understanding the words which they encountered. Gardette further described his school days by recounting the mathematical lessons given by Neef:

Great blackboards hung in the school-rooms, and the method of indoor instruction was as follows: Arithmetic, for instance, being the matter in hand, and the rule of three (the highest point I ever reached while there) the special problem, a boy was chosen from the class, who chalked upon the board, such a statement as 4:16 :: 7:28, and having given the proof in the peculiar manner adopted by Neef and explained in his book, he called the statement and the demonstration aloud, and the entire class repeated them after him, over and over, till they were finally impressed upon their minds. The power of memory—especially for numbers—obtained by the pupils in this way was quite remarkable. Little boys of ten or twelve would multiply thousands by tens of thousands, promptly, without slate or pencil, or give correct answers in the rule of three, no matter how great the figures, as quickly as you could have worked it out on paper.[19]

Neef frequently took the students on field excursions to give them direct contact with nature. During these short trips, the students observed nature and collected plants, small animals, and minerals which were taken to the school and used as objects of further study. Neef indicated the practical uses which could be made of these natural objects. These field trips not only acquainted the students with the various economic occupations being pursued in the vicinity of the school but also provided physical exercise. According to Gardette:

Our outdoor life was equally curious. We never wore hats, Winter or Summer, and many of us went barefooted, also during warm weather.

Our master, hatless as ourselves, would lead us on long tramps through the adjacent country, talking, as we went, upon agriculture, botany, mineralogy, and the like, in a pleasantly descriptive way, and pointing out to us their practical illustration in the grain fields, the gardens, the rocks and streams along our route. And wherever we came we were always recognized, by our bare heads and hardy habits, as the "Neef boys from the Falls."[20]

Neef was one of the early advocates of planned physical education and actually provided for it in his curriculum. His students participated in physical activities, athletics, and sports. Like Pestalozzi, Neef believed that specially graduated exercises would develop man's physical potentiality, strengthen the body, and provide preparation for occupational life. As a result of his soldiering with Napoleon's army, Neef found that physical training was needed for military skill and discipline. He encouraged military drill and vigorously combative physical activities, such as wrestling. When criticized, Neef argued that every youth should be able to defend himself. In recalling these activities, Gardette said:

We were encouraged in all athletic sports, were great swimmers and skaters, walkers and gymnasts. In the pleasant weather we went to bathe twice every day in the Schuylkill, with Neef, who was an accomplished swimmer, at our Head.[21]

Finally, Neef cultivated a permissive student-teacher relationship at his school. Although Pestalozzi considered himself a kindly father to his students, Neef always wanted to be a fellow learner along with them. Neef's practice in the school at the Falls conformed to his stated promise of never being "grave, doctorial, magisterial, and dictatorial."[22] Gardette supplied a clear picture of Neef as a man and as a teacher:

It was, possibly, owing to these amusements and exercises being taken in common with our master, that there existed between Neef and his pupils a freedom so great as to be sometimes, I fear, slightly inconsistent with good breeding or the deference due from pupil to teacher. But this seemed to be part of the system, and Mr. Neef was a thoroughly good-tempered, simple-mannered and amiable man, without an atom of false pride or pedagogism. At the period I speak of, he may have been forty years of age. Though possessing agreeable manners and many accomplishments, Mr. Neef had no inclination for society, and on the few occasions when it became necessary that he should visit the city, his wife, an excellent and notable woman, would tie a cravat (which he habitually went without) round his neck, and clap a hat on his head, much to his disgust and annoyance.[23]

Neef's school, located at the Falls of the Schuylkill from 1809 until 1812, seems to have been successful. His students numbered at least seventy-five and some accounts indicate an enrollment of more than one hundred. Then, for some unaccounted reason, Neef transferred the school to a town known variously as Falling Stars or Village Green.

School at Village Green   Neef was reluctant to remain long in any one place and frequently moved his schools. He operated the school at Village Green, from 1813 until 1815, and was beset with financial difficulties, declining enrollments, and public controversy. At Village Green, Neef continued to use the Pestalozzian method that had been followed at the Falls of the Schuylkill. Within the context of a permissive educational environment, object lessons, physical education, nature study, and field excursions were part of the school routine. It was at Village Green that Neef taught his most famous student, David Glasgow Farragut, who was destined for a distinguished career as an admiral in the United States Navy.[24] After serving as a midshipman in the War of 1812, Farragut, aged thirteen, was enrolled in July 1814 in Neef's school by his guardian, Captain David Porter. Farragut, in the school for only five months, was withdrawn in November 1814 upon receipt of orders recalling him to service. Lewis, Farragut's biographer, wrote that young David Glasgow was left under the tutelage of an

. . . odd old fellow named Neif [sic], who had been one of the celebrated guards of Napoleon Bonaparte. His pupils had no books, but were taught orally on various subjects, taking notes on which they were afterwards examined. In the afternoon he usually took them on long walks, during which Neif added to his collections of minerals and plants and talked to his scholars about mineralogy and botany. They were taught to swim and climb, and were drilled like soldiers.[25]

Although with Neef for only a few months, Farragut gained a great deal of useful information and worldly knowledge from this experience. Despite the irregularity of the course of study, Farragut later said, "I do not regret the time passed at this school for it has been of service to me all through life."[26]

Neef, who consistently refused to teach any particular religious dogma or doctrine, became embroiled in religious controversy at Village Green. His *Sketch* had indicated that he would stress a rational morality, not based upon any particular sectarian tenets, but common to all religious and ethical systems.[27] Because of his unwillingness to indoctrinate his students, Neef was labeled as an atheist who sought to corrupt the morals of youth.

Neef's opponents also charged him with employing a "bad" pedagogical method. Admittedly for the early nineteenth century, Neef's pedagogy was as unconventional as his unorthodox religious views. He refused to use the catechism to instill religious values; he rejected an exclusively literary conception of education; and, like his patron William Maclure, he believed that education should have practical rather than ornamental consequences. In a letter to Neef, Maclure referred to the "cabal" in Philadelphia which opposed both Neef's school and the introduction of Pestalozzianism. Maclure indicated that the charges alleging Neef used a "bad method" or taught "immorality" were merely subterfuges contrived to mask the privileged classes' fear that the productive working classes might seek the power which was rightfully theirs.

. . . You must not believe that the opposition to your school is from a conviction that it is a bad method—on the contrary those who had the cabal are well aware of the ease and certainty with which all useful knowledge can be given and only tremble for the monopoly which is become necessary to their existence. It is not because you teach immorality as they pretend to say but because you take the shortest and surest road to knowledge without the poison of prejudice that they see in you an enemy to their privilege and assumed superiority.[28]

Maclure, who believed that knowledge, power, and freedom were intimately related, encouraged Neef to persist in his efforts at popularizing Pestalozzianism. According to Maclure's views, the inadequately educated working classes had allowed the consuming, nonproducing classes to monopolize wealth, power, and education. While neglecting the poor, the nonproducing classes had established universities, colleges, and seminaries to educate their own children.[29] If the working classes were given a utilitarian education, Maclure believed that they could be prepared to use their economic and political power to overturn the privileged monopoly who had victimized them. Maclure and Neef, as well as Pestalozzi, were aware of class rivalries and believed education to be the means of achieving peaceful change. Although he desired to join an agricultural institute to Neef's school at Village Green, Maclure feared this venture might engender still more controversy and ruin the work already done. Maclure's plan for an agricultural school was deferred until he later incorporated agriculture into the curriculum of the New Harmony schools.

Although Neef had indicated his intention to train teachers in the Pestalozzian method, this was never done on any significant scale.[30] Maclure approved of Neef's decision to restrict enrollment to only those students he could teach himself. Other than for some minimum assistance from the older students, Neef was the only teacher.[31] Both Neef and Maclure knew that dissension among the conflicting camps of teachers was destroying Pestalozzi's institute at Yverdon. Neef's failure to train a number of assistants in Pestalozzian pedagogy weakened the diffusion of that method in the United States in the early years of the nineteenth century. Neef might have had a greater impact on the course of American educational history if he had followed Pestalozzi's example of preparing enough disciples to perpetuate and diffuse his educational theory.

Neef Moves to Kentucky   With the Village Green school plagued by controversy, declining enrollments, and financial losses, Neef in 1815 decided to leave Pennsylvania for Louisville, Kentucky, where he again tried to establish a Pestalozzian school; but the effort was so shortlived that no trace remains of it. Neef also lost money in litigation regarding title to property that he had purchased in Louisville.[32] On May 23, 1816, Maclure wrote to Neef that he was becoming increasingly pessimistic about the possibilities of diffusing Pestalozzianism in the United States.[33] Only ten years before, Neef and Maclure had negotiated an agreement in a spirit of optimism. Maclure had then confidently affirmed his belief that the United States, with its republican self-government, represented an environment which was open to the growth of Pestalozzi's system of natural education. After some initial success, both men were now thoroughly discouraged. Maclure felt that Neef's move to Kentucky would impede the establishment of industrial schools for the working class because a slave state, like Kentucky, would be sterile ground for the growth of Pestalozzianism.[34]

Thoroughly discouraged, Neef abandoned his educational efforts in 1821 and turned to farming. Five years later he was still trying to earn a livelihood from his one-hundred-acre Kentucky farm. Not until 1826 did Neef again join forces with Maclure to renew the efforts initiated twenty years earlier at their first meeting in Paris.

3

NEW HARMONY: A DESIGN FOR UTOPIA

In 1826, Joseph Neef joined Robert Owen's brief but historically significant communitarian social experiment at New Harmony, Indiana. Owen's "Community of Equality" has long intrigued American intellectual, social, and educational historians who have been drawn to the bewildering maze of diverse sources which are the remnants of this utopian experiment.[1] In *Backwoods Utopias*, Arthur Bestor called the coming of Robert Owen, William Maclure, Thomas Say, Joseph Neef, and others to New Harmony "one of the significant intellectual migrations of history."[2] Scientists, naturalists, and educators were transported to the Indiana frontier. In New Harmony's schools, Maclure, Neef, Madame Fretageot and other educators sought to found an outpost of Pestalozzian pedagogy.

Although the Owenite experiment lasted less than two years, Neef was the major Pestalozzian teacher in the New Harmony schools established by his friend and patron, William Maclure. Neef, too, was optimistic that Owen's community would be the portent of a new social order in which, perhaps, Pestalozzianism might be firmly established at last. When the experiment degenerated into contentious factionalism, he must have been deeply disillusioned.

Although he was the principal Pestalozzian teacher in New Harmony's schools, Neef was secondary to the primary figures of the experiment, Robert Owen and William Maclure. The plan to create a utopia on the American frontier was Owen's, and it was Maclure who promised to establish a system of Pesta-lozzian schools to educate the children of these utopians. Neef's educational work at New Harmony must be interpreted, there-fore, in the context created by these primary personalities. Since Neef was only one of many educators who came to New Harmony at Maclure's request, Neef's specific educational endeavors must be considered in terms of Maclure's pedagogial plans.

Robert Owen's Experiment   On April 27, 1825, Robert Owen, English industrialist, educator, philanthropist, and utopian socialist, purchased the Posey County town of New Harmony, Indiana, from the Rappites, a communal sect of pietistical Prot-estants who had come to the United States from Württemberg, Germany.[3] The success of Owen's model factory community at New Lanark in Scotland had made him a public personage. At New Lanark, Owen had established a community school which emphasized permissiveness, sensory training, and activities rather than language learning. When Owen decided to transfer his philanthropic activity to the United States, which he be-lieved would be more hospitable to social innovation than tra-dition-bound England, he saw New Harmony as a model com-munity, a beacon, which would illuminate a vast social reform program. In 1824, Owen made his first trip to the United States to inspect the Rappite property at New Harmony. He visited several educational institutions, among them those conducted by associates of William Maclure.[4] In Philadelphia, Owen called at the school of Madame Marie Duclos Fretageot, whom Maclure had brought to the United States as a Pestalozzian teacher.

Owen's enthusiasm for his project was contagious, and he in-spired Madame Fretageot, who, in turn, persuaded Maclure to join the utopian venture. Maclure had returned to the United States after the restoration of the "old regime" in Spain had forced the abandonment of his project of establishing an agri-cultural school at Alcinate. He was already familiar with Owen since he had visited New Lanark in 1824. Although the educa-tional and social reforms at New Lanark impressed him, Maclure was reluctant to commit himself and his money to Owen's uto-pian scheme.[5] While sympathetic to humanitarian reform,

Maclure felt that Owen's design was hastily contrived, poorly developed, and overly optimistic. He was convinced that genuine social reform would come only gradually as generations of children were educated according to Pestalozzi's natural method.

After settling his affairs in England, Owen returned to the United States in November 1825 and met with Maclure. Owen's infectious enthusiasm and the persuasion of Madame Fretageot, Phiquepal d'Arusmont, and Thomas Say finally convinced Maclure to join the New Harmony venture. Although both Owen and Maclure agreed to cooperate, spheres of authority were not clearly defined, nor were financial liabilities specifically determined. These vague arrangements later produced a law suit which embarrassed both philanthropists. It was generally assumed that Owen would direct the entire community while Maclure organized the schools. During these preliminary meetings, Neef was still trying to eke out a living on his unprosperous Kentucky farm. Soon after committing himself to Owen's plan, Maclure wrote Neef and encouraged him to sell his farm, come to New Harmony, and organize the schools according to the Pestalozzian principles he knew so well.

New Harmony as a Communitarian Experiment   Neef's educational work at New Harmony can be evaluated only within the communitarian context which was basic to the experiment. According to Bestor, "communitarian" and "communitarianism" are "derived immediately from community, and they signify primarily a system of social reform based on small communities."[6] In discussing the common factor which characterized nineteenth century American communitarianism, Bestor has written:

What these enterprises had in common was the idea of employing the small experimental community as a lever to exert upon society the force necessary to produce reform and change. The ends might differ, with economic, religious, ethical, and educational purposes mingled in varying proportions. But the means were uniform, consistent, and well defined. These enterprises constituted a communitarian movement because each made the community the heart of its plan.[7]

Most communitarians believed that the small, voluntary, experimental community would effect the immediate reform of its residents. Since this social regeneration was to be accomplished peacefully, education was relied upon as the chief instrument of reform. Once established, the model community would radiate waves of reform. In order to reap the benefits of communitarian life, other individuals would organize their own communities in emulation of the successful example.

Since Pestalozzi believed that permanent personal and social regeneration could be secured through education, his sociological and pedagogical theories were adaptable to the communitarian impulse.[8] Pestalozzi's own book, *Leonard and Gertrude*, told of the social redemption of a village of simple Swiss peasants by the means of natural education. To such convinced Pestalozzians as Maclure and Neef, Owen's experimental community was a proper environment for establishing the natural system of education.

It was not surprising that the educational efforts of the New Harmony reformers were bound inextricably to their particular social, political, and economic beliefs. Robert Owen's reform program at New Lanark used education to improve the living conditions of his textile workers. William Maclure believed that utilitarian education would liberate the energy of the working masses and enable them to secure political power. Joseph Neef believed that a rational system of education would produce intelligent self-governing republican citizens. In commenting on the reciprocity that existed between the communitarians and the educational reformers of the nineteenth century, Bestor has clearly related education to its social context:

More remarkable even than the communitarian's interest in education was the complementary tendency of educational reformers to think in communitarian terms. To begin with, schoolmen of the early nineteenth century were giving increased attention to the social context of education. So long as this wider outlook inspired no more than an adjustment of the curriculum to changes in society, it had few implications for the reform movement generally. But there were educationists to whom the relationship between school and society appeared a reciprocal one. The school should respond to social change, they held, but it should also be an instrument for effecting desirable alterations in society. In their hands educational reform became a branch of social reform.[9]

The New Harmony educators aptly fit Bestor's description of the alliance between educational reformer and communitarian. Pestalozzi, himself, had examined the sociological bases of education as he worked to devise his natural educational method. Pestalozzi regarded education as the means of developing man's moral, intellectual, and physical powers. As such, it was the chief instrument in cultivating the harmoniously functioning natural man. For Pestalozzi, however, individual reformation was prior to social reform. While society could not make men good, naturally educated individuals could fashion a moral society.

Robert Owen conceived social reconstruction to be a total process. He believed that the community, as an informal educational agency, was a more potent force for securing societal reform than the formal school, itself. As an educational agency in the broad sense, the successful model community would inspire the estabishment of other communities according to the design which had produced the paradigm. Owen saw the school as a formal institution that would reflect the reformed values that had already been established within the community. While the school could not create the new society, it would perpetuate the new social design by transmitting communitarian knowledge, skills, and values to succeeding generations.

William Maclure, director of the New Harmony schools, relied more on the formal educative process as a means of reform than did Owen. Pessimistic about adult reformation, Maclure believed that genuine social change would occur as children were educated according to natural and utilitarian methods. He remained true to his conviction that Pestalozzianism was the ideal educational method to accomplish the social reformation of mankind.

As a teacher, Joseph Neef directed his efforts more to the processes of formal schooling than did either of the far-ranging theorists, Owen or Maclure. A republican committed to individualism, Neef believed that men who were educated rationally could produce a rational society. Although a firm individualist, Neef rejected the social artificialities which private property had produced and believed that communal ownership would restore man's natural equality.

The questions raised by Owen, Maclure, and Neef regarding the reconstructive role of the school were not unique to the early nineteenth century. During the depression of the 1930's, certain American educational theorists explored much the same ground. In 1932, George S. Counts raised the issue of the school's responsibility for social reform when he asked, *Dare the School Build a New Social Order?*[10] Theodore Brameld has credited Owen's work as being a significant forerunner to his own educational philosophy of social reconstructionism.[11] The transition from pedagogue to reformer suggests that an interesting parallel may exist between the nineteenth century communitarians at New Harmony and the twentieth century social reconstructionist educators. Although Owen, Maclure, and Neef initially sought to liberalize school practice by making it more responsive to the child's nature, interests, and needs, they eventually used their reformed pedagogy as an instrument for social reform. Many of the twentieth century social reconstructionists had participated in the progressive education movement and had opposed traditional school practices which restricted the child's freedom. During the Depression, the reconstructionists came to believe that progressive educators, by concentrating exclusively on the child, had ignored pressing social issues. They then began to urge that formal education be used to fashion a cooperative society.[12]

New Harmony as an Experiment in Popular Education   Some interpreters of Neef's educational work have indicated that he was too far ahead of his times. Since the common school movement led by Horace Mann and Henry Barnard did not gain momentum until the late 1830's and 1840's, no institutionalized educational establishment existed to serve as a springboard for the popularization of Pestalozzianism. Many of the existing schools, maintained under religious auspices, were unlikely to accept Neef's "free-thinking" rationalism.

The schools which comprised Maclure's educational system at New Harmony can be viewed in several ways: one, as instruments of social reform; two, as vehicles for diffusing Pestalozzianism; three, as practical and utilitarian industrial institutions; four, as isolated prototypes of the common school. In terms of the latter, the efforts of Neef and Maclure anticipated Mann's common-school crusade for popular education. New Harmony's schools, like the later nineteenth century common school, were nonsectarian institutions open to all the children in the community.

Although bearing some similarities to the common-school movement, the embryonic experiment in popular education at New Harmony represented a more basic shift in educational theory and practice. The Harmonist revolt against classical learning was also a rebellion against a society dominated by the vested interests of both conservative, aristocratic southern planters and laissez-faire, northern capitalists. This anticlassicalist and unconventional educational experiment conducted on the American frontier was really intended to effect a peaceful revolution on behalf of agricultural and industrial working classes.

Maclure, Owen, and Neef rejected the classical humanist Greek and Latin language curriculum as an outdated educational survival which had been made obsolete by scientific knowledge and industrial needs. While liberal businessmen could conceivably share this anticlassical bias, they could not agree with communitarian antipathy to private property and profit. Owen, Maclure, and Neef advocated popular education as a nonviolent means of ameliorating the exploitation of the workingmen during the harsh and dehumanizing stages of early industrialization. Their educational efforts were directed not only to practical and utilitarian ends but also at basic socioeconomic-political reform.

In contrast to New Harmony's utopian socialists, the common-school leaders, Mann and Barnard, enlisted the support of businessmen in behalf of universal, popular education. Holding that wealth was produced by applying social intelligence to the exploitation of natural resources, Mann told businessmen that this investment in common schooling could increase both social intelligence and material prosperity. Commenting on Barnard's strong inclination to ally popular education with private property, Merle Curti has written: ". . . He seems to have sanctioned what was virtually the indoctrination of the teachers of youth with capitalistic theory."[13] While Mann and Barnard used common schooling to minimize socioeconomic class differences, Maclure and Neef conceived of popular education as an instrument of freeing the working class from domination by the upper class.

In the early twentieth century, United States Commissioner of Education William T. Harris, a staunch defender of the public school's alliance with corporate industry, clearly distinguished between these differing conceptions of popular education. In criticizing Robert Dale Owen's efforts on behalf of public school legislation in Indiana, Harris clearly preferred the strategy of Mann and Barnard. According to Harris:

If Robert Dale Owen had described the true effects of school education in the line of freedom of property and independent initiative, he would have recommended his scheme for free public schools more effectively than he was able to do as the representative of a communistic experiment, for his communism preached a silent lesson in contradiction to his plea for free schools.[14]

New Harmony as a Community of Equality   The New Harmony communitarians opposed private property ownership as the source of human and social evil. They believed that common property and popular education would be the "great equalizers" which would destory the impediments to progress produced by unequal social classes, ranks, and distinctions. On May 1, 1825, the "Preliminary Society of New Harmony" formed "to improve the character and conditions of its own members, and to prepare them to become associates in independent communities, having common property."[15] Ten months later, on February 5, 1826, an overly optimistic Robert Owen proclaimed the "Community of Equality." The Constitution adopted by the community members revealed their basic social and educational convictions as they committed themselves to an "equality of rights" and "equality of duties" within the communal context of "cooperative union" and a "community of property." According to the Constitution:

... Man's character, mental, moral, and physical, is the result of his formation, his location, and ... the circumstances within which he exists.

***

... man is powerful in action, efficient in production, and happy in social life, only as he acts cooperatively and unitedly.

***

All members of the community shall be considered as one family, and no one shall be held in higher or lower estimation on account of occupation. There shall be similar food, clothing, and education, as near as can be furnished, for all according to their ages; and, as soon as practicable, all shall live in similar houses, and in all respects be accomodated alike. Every member shall render his or her best services for the good of the whole, according to the rules and regulations that may be hereafter adopted by the community. It shall always remain a primary object of the community to give the best physical, moral, and intellectual education to all its members.[16]

New Harmony's Constitution was a typical restatement of Robert Owen's views on property, community, environment, and education. Property was to be held in common by the community. Man was a product of his environment, and an environment of private ownership made man selfish and egotistical. In contrast, individuals living in a communal environment would willingly work for the good of the entire community. Free for all citizens, the schools would reflect and transmit communitarian values and ensure the perpetuation of the "Community of Equality."

Many of Joseph Neef's ideas were parallel to, rather than derived from, Owen's social philosophy. He agreed with Owen's condemnation of private property. While aware of the impact of environment in forming human character, Neef was not a simple determinist but believed that man's rationality enabled him to transcend environmental limitations. Despite these areas of theoretical agreement, Neef disliked Owen's practices and later accused him of being unfaithful to his own system and of causing the failure of the New Harmony experiment.

Maclure's Boatload of Knowledge   Although agreeing to co-operate with Owen, Maclure did not abandon his educational objectives of popularizing Pestalozzianism and of establishing agricultural and industrial schools. Maclure wanted to bring his intellectual associates to New Harmony as the nucleus of a major scientific and educational center. While teaching in the schools, this group could engage in scientific and peda-gogical research. In time, their contributions could be dissem-inated across the United States. Maclure sent his extensive li-brary, scientific instruments, and natural history collection to the Indiana village and then gathered together the individuals who would aid him in his plans.

Maclure wanted his old friend and associate, Joseph Neef, to be a leading member of his New Harmony educational center. Neef, who had abandoned teaching, was still working his small farm near Floydsburg in Kentucky. Since the New Harmony schools were to follow Pestalozzian principles, Maclure be-lieved Neef to be the ideal person to assist him in organizing the educational system. He wrote to Neef and urged him to come to New Harmony where his invaluable assistance was needed in this noble experiment of human reformation.[17]

Maclure gathered his band of intellectuals at Philadelphia for the journey to the Indiana frontier. At Pittsburgh, he pur-chased a keelboat aptly named the *Philanthropist,* and the group embarked on the Ohio for the last stage of their journey. Robert Owen referred to this migration of Maclure's circle of Phila-delphia intellectuals as the "boatload of knowledge." Although Neef was not aboard the *Philanthropist,* most of his associates in the New Harmony schools were present. With Owen and Maclure were Thomas Say and Charles Lesueur, naturalists; Marie Duclos Fretageot and Phiquepal d'Arusmont, Pestalozzian teachers; Gerard Troost, a Dutch mineralogist; Robert Dale Owen, the son of the project's originator; Captain Donald Macdonald, a friend of Owen and a former English army officer; and Stedman Whitwell, architect.[18]

Aboard the *Philanthropist* were the nucleus of the Education Society and general faculty of New Harmony's schools. Some, like Troost, were close friends of Neef, and others, like Madame Fretageot, would become his enemies. Since they were to work with Neef, a brief discussion of the backgrounds and careers of some of the more significant figures will shed further light on subsequent events which occurred at New Harmony.

Thomas Say, 1787–1834, a native Philadelphian, was a lifelong friend and associate of Maclure. A charter member of the Academy of Natural Science, Say devoted his energies to collecting, describing, and cataloguing American fauna.[19] He accompanied Maclure on scientific expeditions to Florida in 1817 and the Georgia islands in 1818. Say was the chief zoologist with Major Stephen Long's Rocky Mountain expedition in 1819. While at New Harmony, Say assisted in the schools where he lectured on natural history. His minor writings were *American Entomology*, 1817, and the three volume *American Entomology*, 1824–1828. During his frequent absences from New Harmony, Maclure placed Say in charge of the educational activities. More interested in his research Say was a poor administrator.

Gerard Troost, 1776–1850, a Dutch mineralogist, was a co-founder of the Academy of Natural Sciences in Philadelphia, serving as President from 1812 to 1817. He had been a mineralogy professor at the Philadelphia Museum and a professor of chemistry at the Philadelphia College of Pharmacy before coming to New Harmony. Like Say, Troost lectured on natural history in the New Harmony schools. Troost was a close friend of Neef and publicly defended him against charges of incompetence. After Owen's experiment disintegrated, Troost moved to Nashville, Tennessee, where he taught chemistry, geology, and mineralogy. From 1831 to 1839, he was the Tennessee State Geologist.[20]

Charles Alexander Lesueur, 1778–1846, a French artist and zoologist, came to the United States in 1815 at Maclure's urging. He taught drawing and painting in Philadelphia and gave art instructions in Madame Fretageot's Pestalozzian school. Lesueur wrote the first classifications of the fish in the Great Lakes and also published an account of the primitive Indiana mound builders. At Maclure's request, he reluctantly joined the intellectual migration to New Harmony and taught in the schools during Owen's experiment. He was a friend of Say, whose works he illustrated. In 1836, he returned to France to accept the directorship of the museum at Le Havre.[21]

Marie Louise Duclos Fretageot, also a native of France, was another of the Pestalozzian teachers whom Maclure had brought to the United States. In November 1821, she opened a Pestalozzian school in Philadelphia which attracted sufficient attention to merit a visit from Robert Owen in 1824. She was so impressed by Owen's plan for educational and social reform at New Harmony that she persuaded Maclure to join the venture. She conducted one of the New Harmony schools but did not get along with Neef, and the two had a running quarrel which Maclure unsuccessfully tried to mediate. When the Owenite community collapsed, she remained in New Harmony to administer's Maclure's interests. From 1826 to 1831, she directed many of the scientific and educational activities at New Harmony. She died in Mexico in 1833, where she had gone to visit Maclure.

Robert Dale Owen, 1801–1877, came with his father to New Harmony, taught in the schools, and helped to edit the *Gazette*. His attendance at Emmanuel Fellenberg's school at Hofwyl and familiarity with his father's school at New Lanark gave him a lasting interest in education. As a teacher, young Owen came to know and respect Neef, whom he regarded as a blunt but capable person. He later entered Indiana politics and served in the state legislature from 1836 to 1842, in the United States Congress from 1842 to 1847, and in the Indiana Constitutional Convention in 1850. An inveterate reformer like his father, he proposed legislation for women's rights, free schools, abolition of slavery, and for the creation of the Smithsonian Institution. The last years of his life were devoted to investigating and advancing his interest in spiritualism.[22]

Phiquepal d'Arusmont was still another Pestalozzian teacher whom Maclure had induced to come to Philadelphia. In 1824, he had just established his Pestalozzian school for boys when he was called upon to join the migration to New Harmony. At New Harmony, d'Arusmont had difficulty in cooperating with the other teachers. Robert Dale Owen, who believed that d'Arusmont's egotism destroyed his usefulness as an educator, called him a "wrong-headed genius."[23] He later married Frances Wright, an early feminist, abolitionist, and founder of the Nashoba colony in Tennessee. Frances Wright was herself a frequent visitor to New Harmony during Owen's experiment.

Meeting the *Philanthropist* at Louisville, Neef conferred with Maclure, and agreed to sell his unprosperous farm and join the New Harmony community. When he had difficulty in arranging his affairs in Kentucky, Maclure again wrote to Neef, on February 20, 1826, urging him to hasten to New Harmony, where matters affecting the schools were still being debated by the members of Owen's community. Maclure told Neef that his frontier experience and skill as a Pestalozzian teacher were needed if the schools were to function properly.[24] On March 20, 1826, Neef finally arrived at New Harmony and began his active work in the educational system.

Although Neef would be involved in his work at New Harmony for only two years, it was a stimulating and challenging period for him. He worked with some of the leading scientists, naturalists, and educators of the time. As is frequently the case with intellectuals, more time was spent on theoretical arguments and petty egotistical contentions than on the actual enterprise. Neef fully participated in this experiment in American communitarianism and joined in many of the controversies which beset the "Community of Equality."

4

NEW HARMONY EDUCATION

Even before the arrival of Maclure's Pestalozzian educators, New Harmony's Preliminary Society had committed the community to popular education. Its Constitution, adopted in 1825, pledged that education, a public property, would be open to all the community's children. By December 1825 one hundred and forty students were attending the schools, which were being temporarily directed by William Owen and Robert Jennings. Although these schools were open to all New Harmony's residents, nonresident students were accepted upon application and an annual payment of one hundred dollars for board, lodging, washing, clothing, medical care, and tuition. True to Robert Owen's belief in equality of opportunity regardless of sex, girls had the same educational advantages as boys.

On January 26, 1826, the "boatload of knowledge" reached New Harmony. Maclure took charge of the community's schools and began to implement his design for industrial education according to Pestalozzian principles. Maclure recognized that the application of science to agriculture and industry had changed the means of production. He had developed his own sociological theory, which held that society was divided into two great classes: the unproductive consumers and the producing farmers and laborers. All of his sympathies were with the producing classes, which he believed to be victimized by exploiting landowners and capitalists. Education, he felt, had not kept pace with the basic scientific and industrial transformations which were beginning to change western culture. Formal schooling was still impractical, classical, verbal, unscientific, nonutilitarian, and ornamental. Although the unproductive upper classes might waste their time and money on Latin and Greek, the producers needed a sound, practical, industrial, and scientific education.

Since he believed Pestalozzianism to be the most useful, practical, and efficient means of instruction yet devised, Maclure decided to employ this method in advancing his plan of industrial education. He sought out a number of skilled Pestalozzian teachers and brought them from Europe to introduce the method to Americans. Neef was the earliest arrival, and his schools in Pennsylvania were the first to practice Pestalozzianism in the United States.

As a student of Pestalozzianism, Maclure believed that education should be based on sensation; instruction was to be gradual, orderly, and progressive; children were not to be taught words which they did not fully understand. Following Pestalozzi's specifications, instruction would proceed from the known to the unknown, the easy to the difficult, the simple to the complex, and the particular to the general. Above all, Maclure wanted his teachers to base their instruction on the empirical and avoid the errors caused by untested imagination. When Maclure announced his program of education for the New Harmony schools in the *American Journal of Sciences and Arts,* it read like a page from Neef's own *Sketch.* According to Maclure:

The great or fundamental principle is, never attempt to teach children what they do not comprehend, and to teach them in the exact ratio of their understanding without omitting one link in the chain of ratiocination, proceeding always from the known to the unknown, from the most easy to the most difficult; practising the most extensive and accurate use of all the senses; exercising, improving, and perfecting all the mental and corporeal faculties by quickening combination; accelerating and carefully arranging comparisons; judiciously and impartially making deductions; summing up the results free from prejudices, and cautiously avoiding the delusions of imagination, a constant source of ignorance and error.[1]

The New Harmony School System   The New Harmony educational system consisted of three institutions: an infant, a
higher, and an adult school. At its peak, the infant school enrolled more than one hundred children from ages two to five.
After Neef's arrival on March 20, 1826, his wife Eloisa shared
instruction in the infant school with Madame Fretageot. Mrs.
Neef had been educated in Pestalozzi's school at Burgdorf, and
Madame Fretageot had conducted a Pestalozzian school in
Philadelphia. The operations of the infant school were impaired
when antagonistic rivalry developed between the two Pestalozzians, Joseph Neef and Marie Duclos Fretageot. Although
Maclure tried to mediate the controversy, Madame Fretageot
was unable to cooperate with Neef. She withdrew some of the
students and established a separate school in New Harmony's
building number five. No longer concentrating exclusively on
early childhood education, she taught students of all ages. In
commenting on her work she wrote:

I get up at four o'clock regularly and have a class of twelve young
men until six-thirty. They go to work at seven. Breakfast at eight.
Nine to eleven, the class of children under twelve. At two, the same
children until four. At six, and until eight, all the children above
twelve. I leave the piano and go to the kitchen, as I have no cook. The
other hours I am occupied looking for the whole family. I may say
that I have very little occasion for wearing out the chairs of the house,
having not a single female to help me.[2]

While Madame Fretageot was an efficient and accomplished
woman, the duplication of educational efforts caused by maintaining separate schools weakened the school system. Unfortunately, this duplication also ended the brief existence of the
infant school. This institution might have proved to be an interesting combination of Owenite and Pestalozzian educational
theory. Robert Owen, a pioneer in early childhood education,
had established an infant school at New Lanark. Since he believed that man's character was environmentally determined,
Owen began education as early as possible. At New Lanark,
children had entered the infant school at age two in order to

experience the effects of a properly prepared educational environment. Owen's New Lanark school gave no instruction in reading, writing, or other verbal skills, nor were there predetermined lessons or punishments. While objects were used in instruction, they remained unexplained until the child's own curiosity led him to conduct his own investigation. During the New Harmony experiment, Owen was so obsessed with diverse plans and preachments for social reform that he failed to create the same kind of infant school which had contributed to New Lanark's fame.

Joseph Neef was superintendent of the higher school which enrolled approximately two hundred students, ranging in age from five through twelve. As the community boarding school, Neef's higher school served the educational needs of both the community children and a number of nonresident students who came to New Harmony for the distinctive type of education which Maclure had outlined in the *American Journal of Sciences and Arts*. The higher school was the most distinctively Pestalozzian of all the educational enterprises at New Harmony. Neef was, of course, a committed Pestalozzian who adapted the method to conform to Maclure's views of an industrial education suited to the socioeconomic needs of working class children. Maclure outlined the basic curriculum which Neef offered in the higher school:

The children are to learn mechanism by machines or exact modes of them, arithmetic by a machine called the arithmometer, geometry by a machine called the trignometer, by which the most useful propositions of Euclid are reduced to the comprehension of a child five or six years old; mathematics by the help of the above-mentioned instruments.
Natural history . . . is learned by examining objects in substance or accurate representations of them in designs or prints; anatomy by skeletons and wax figures; geography by globes and maps—most of the last by their own construction; hygiene . . . by their own experience and observation of . . . natural functions. They learn natural philosophy by the most improved and simple instruments.
They are taught writing and designing by the freedom of hand acquired by constant practise in forming . . . figures with a slate and pencil . . . when they first enter the school, on which they draw lines,

dividing them into equal parts, thereby obtaining an accuracy of the eye which, joined to the constant exercise of judging the distance of objects and their height, gives them a perfect idea of space.

They learn music through the medium of an organ constructed for the purpose, and a sonometer, first learning the sounds and then the notes, or signs of those sounds.

Gymnastics . . . they acquire by the practice of all kinds of movements always, preferably, those that may lead to utility, such as marching, climbing, the manual exercises, *etc.* They are taught the greatest part of these branches at the same time, never fatiguing the mind by giving more than an hour's attention to the same thing, changing the subject and rendering it play by variety.

The pupils learn as many languages as there are languages spoken by the boys of different nations . . . each instructing the other . . . in his language.

Lithographing and engraving as well as printing are . . . carried on in the school building, as well as other mechanic arts, that the children may receive manual training. The boys learn at least one mechanical art—for instance, setting type and printing, and for this purpose there are printing-presses in each school by the aid of which are published all their elementary books.[3]

In following Maclure's curriculum, Neef gave instruction in useful occupations and trades. Each child was to choose his own occupation. When unable to make such a choice, he was assigned to a trade. Such vocational courses as taxidermy, printing, engraving, drawing, carpentry, wheelwrighting, woodturning, blacksmithing, cabinet making, hat making, shoemaking, washing, cooking, sewing, housekeeping, dressmaking, and millinery were taught. The students did not return to their homes but slept in a dormitory above the school.[4]

Maclure believed that such industrial schools could eventually become self-sustaining. As the students learned trades, the income derived from the sale of their products could be used to support the school. Pestalozzi originally believed in the possibility of establishing self-supporting educational institutions. His first school at Neuhof had unsuccessfully combined agriculture, spinning, and basic education. During his later career, Pestalozzi minimized the overtly vocational aspects of his educational program and emphasized the more general features of natural education. Maclure, on the other hand, was always keenly interested in establishing self-supporting institutions, in which children could learn a trade, pay for their own education, and gain self-respect. In his earlier Pennsylvania schools, Neef had exposed his students to the various occupations and had examined the uses of natural objects. He did not enter into direct vocational education, however, until he came to New Harmony.

While at New Harmony, Neef still revealed the rationalism which had been so evident in his *Sketch* and in his teaching in the school at the Falls. Although a participant in Owen's plan to create utopia, he did not give way to sentimentalism. He was still the hardheaded, blunt, but kindly realist when he said of his work at New Harmony:

Train a number of boys to gather knowledge by their own senses, to consult experience in every instance, to analyze, to examine, to investigate every thing, to believe nothing. Convince them by their daily experience that the more they trust and believe, the more they are liable to be cheated and imposed upon; the less they believe, the less they will be gulled; and if they believe nothing they will never be deceived; and you will produce men as rational and intelligent as you may wish them to be.[5]

Neef was disappointed with the course of events that occurred at New Harmony and joined Paul Brown and other "self-styled democrats" in criticizing Owen's administration of the community. When he arrived to take charge of the higher school, Neef found that the institution lacked the necessary equipment to function as a boarding school. In later defending himself against charges of administrative incompetence, Neef reminded his critics of the efforts he made to organize an instructional program and to equip the higher school:

Every inhabitant of New Harmony knows that I lost not a moment to organize my department. I had to procure benches and tables for the school rooms, beds and bedsteads for the sleeping rooms, tables and benches for the eating room; forks, knives, plates, cups, in short every article absolutely indispensable for the accommodation of 170 children, the number allotted to my superintendence.—Under every possible disadvantage, which I shall not mention, and which every inhabitant of this place is acquainted with, I began my operations.

My unremitted exertions triumphed over every obstacle, and in two short months, order, regularity, and harmony were established. My children were well classed, their rough edges were wearing off; my teachers began to understand the rationale of my operations; a mutual attachment between the instructors and their pupils was established.[6]

In additon to the infant school and the higher schools, there was Phiquepal d'Arusmont's adult school, the third institution in Maclure's educational system at New Harmony. The adult school enrolled students over the age of twelve and reached an enrollment of eighty. Night classes were given in mathematics, science, and useful arts. Gerard Troost lectured on chemistry, Thomas Say on natural history, and d'Arusmont on experimental farming. Lesueur gave art and drawing lessons. One of the students later reminisced on the adult education program:

One of our teachers, Mr. Lesueur, was a fine artist. He taught drawing and painting, and did a great deal of artistic work outside of the school. He and Thomas Say spent most of their leisure in the woods or in the river searching for shells and catching fish which they painted and described.[7]

During the spring of 1826, Maclure's Educational Society continued to organize and elaborate New Harmony's educational and scientific program. The children enrolled in their schools probably received a better education than that offered in the United States generally. Neef, Fretageot, and d'Arusmont had been specially prepared as teachers. Troost, Say, Lesueur, and others actively engaged in scientific research; their lectures formed an important part of the educational program. Despite these strong features, the schools did not meet Maclure's high expectations. The three Pestalozzian teachers—Neef, Fretageot, and d'Arusmont—were strong individuals who were unable to cooperate. In Maclure's frequent absences, quarrels occurred. Instead of working within the coordinated and articulated school system envisioned by Maclure, each of the three major teachers established a separate school. Their energies were wasted, and the instruction was duplicated. Before turning to these controversies in greater detail, an examination of school life sheds further light on New Harmony's educational system.

School Life at New Harmony   In April 1826, New Harmony
was visited by Karl Bernhard, Duke of Saxe-Weimar Eisanach,
a German aristocrat critical of American egalitarianism and
the "rude people known under the general title of backwoodsmen." Although he disliked Owen's egalitarian theories, Bernhard was fascinated by the New Harmony community. He was
familiar with the educational experiment and with Maclure,
whom he described as a "great adherent of the Pestalozzian
system of education."[8] He recorded his visit to Neef's school:

On the morning of the 14th of April, I strolled about the place to look
round me. I visited Mr. Neef, but found his wife only at home, a native
of Memmingen, in Swabia. Her husband was in the act of leading the
boys out to labour. Military exercises form a part of the instruction
of the children. I saw the boys divided into two ranks, and parted into
detachments marching to labour, and on the way they performed
various wheelings and evolutions. All the boys and girls have a very
healthy look, are cheerful and lively, and by no means bashful. The
boys labour in the field and garden, and were now occupied with new
fencing. The girls learn female employments; they were as little op-
pressed as the boys with labour and teaching; these happy and interesting children were much more employed in making their youth
pass as pleasantly as possible. Madam Neef showed the school-house
in which she dwelt, and in which the places for sleeping were arranged for the boys. Each boy slept on a cot frame, upon a straw bed.[9]

Bernhard's commentary makes it evident that Neef was faithful to his practice of including military drill and formation in
the instructional program. Bernhard described the fifty-six
year old Neef as a "rather aged man." Unappreciative of Neef's
republican predilections, he commented:

I afterwards visited Mr. Neef, who is still full of the maxims and principles of the French revolution; captivated with the system of equality;
talks of the emancipation of the negroes, and openly proclaims himself as an ATHEIST. Such people stand by themselves, and fortunately
are so very few in number, that they can do little or no injury.[10]

Although Bernhard did not like his political and social convictions, he accurately captured Neef's basic beliefs. Neef was
always a convinced republican who tried to incorporate self-

government into his schools. He disliked inequalities, especially those based on blood, birth, and property. Neef abhorred
Negro slavery and probably would have been an abolitionist.
His freethinking religious views had gotten him into difficulty
when he was teaching at Village Green in Pennsylvania.

Robert Dale Owen, the eldest son of Robert Owen, was a
teacher in the New Harmony schools. He was well acquainted
with Neef, whom he called "simple, straightforward, and cordial." Robert Dale Owen found Neef to be proficient in modern
languages, a good musician, an excellent teacher, and a general
favorite of the students. Owen described one amusing incident
which involved Neef:

To his earlier life, as an officer under Napoleon, was due a blunt, off-
hand manner and an abrupt style of speech, enforced now and then,
with an oath—an awkard habit for a teacher, which I think he tried
ineffectually to get rid of. One day, when I was within hearing, a boy
in his class used profane language. "Youngster," said Neef to him,
"you mustn't swear. It's silly, and it's vulgar, and it means nothing.
Don't let me hear you do so again."

"But, Mr. Neef," said the boy, hesitating, and looking half frightened,
"if—if it's vulgar and wrong to swear, why—"

"Well, out with it! Never stop when you want to say anything: that's
another bad habit. You wished to know why—?"

"Why you swear yourself, Mr. Neef?"

"Because I'm a d--d fool. Don't you be one, too."[11]

In contrast to the usual nineteenth century school, the New
Harmony schools were permissive. Maclure and Owen both opposed using corporal punishment and fear to stimulate learning. In his *Sketch*, Neef claimed he would never maintain discipline by corporal punishment or ridicule. In the New Harmony schools, rewards and punishments were abolished except
when arising naturally from the consequences of action. Rather
than fear, Maclure urged his teachers to base motivation on the
learner's interests:

Attention is the only medium through which instruction passes into the mind; without it nothing makes a lasting impression on any of the mental faculties. Can undivided attention be secured by fear or coercion? This is a query necessary to be solved, as a principle upon which education must be bottomed. Does not fear brutalize and paralyze all the faculties of the mind? Let any one at a mature age reflect on his feelings when under the impression of fear and he will find that neither his memory, judgment, nor any other of his mental faculties were sound. Fear perhaps is the great predisposing cause of many both moral and physical diseases.[12]

Neef Opposes a Separate School Society   The New Harmony experiment brought together an unusual mixture of individuals that included unlettered frontiersmen, sophisticated intellectuals, assorted eccentrics, and sheer opportunists. When some of the intellectuals felt themselves hindered by the less educated members of the community, they attempted to organize a separate society, called the "Literati." Although his sons Robert Dale and William were among the Literati, the senior Owen opposed the movement. Maclure proposed a compromise which reorganized the community's population into functional societies based on occupation. On May 28, 1826, three separate societies were formed: an Educational, an Agricultural and Pastoral, and a Mechanic and Manufacturing society.[13] This arrangement was designed to permit Maclure's educational associates to concentrate on the schools while Owen continued his efforts at organizing the whole community.

Neef opposed separating the community into distinct societies and warned Owen and Maclure that this division would factionalize the community. Although he usually agreed with Maclure, Neef opposed him on this occasion. Once the separate society plan was approved, Neef became a member of the Education Society and was its spokesman on several occasions.[14]

Neef–Fretageot Controversy   Although the New Harmony teachers were better prepared than most of their early nineteenth century contemporaries, constant quarreling among the members of the Education Society hindered Maclure's educational plans. By late summer of 1826, Neef, Madame Fretageot, and d'Arusmont were each conducting their own separate schools. D'Arusmont had taken a number of the older boys to his own school in the Steeple house; Neef remained with most of the students in building number two; Madame Fretageot had established her own school in building number five. No longer confining herself to infant education as originally planned, she was now conducting a boarding school for the young men of the community and a day school for children of all ages.[15] Maclure was away at the time when the three Pestalozzian instructors went their separate ways. Although disappointed by the disharmony, Maclure felt that the removal of some students from Neef's school might alleviate overcrowding and facilitate the use of the Pestalozzian method.[16]

The steady stream of correspondence between Maclure and Madame Fretageot provides evidence of the friction which had developed between the Pestalozzian teachers. On August 11, 1826, Madame Fretageot complained that the Neefs were unable to function effectively as administrators of the major school:

... the children under Neef ['s] direction are making progress in every kind of bad habit on account of Neef's sickness and the poor management [of] his wife, that as a housekeeper is the least calculated to be at the head of such an establishment, where order and economy must be the two first principles to be put into practice with the stricktest [sic] attention.[17]

On August 29, Maclure, who was in Cincinnati, wrote to Madame Fretageot and agreed to advise Neef to "be quiet." However, he also restated his loyalty for Neef. Since he was solely responsible for Neef's coming to New Harmony, Maclure announced that he would protect and support Neef's educational plans.[18] The growing animosity between Madame Fretageot and Joseph Neef must have been painful to Maclure, their mutual friend. Neef was the first Pestalozzian teacher whom Maclure had brought to the United States and their association went back twenty years to 1806. Maclure was nevertheless becoming increasingly reliant on the capable, intelligent, and strong-willed Madame Fretageot. Further, Maclure's health began to deteriorate and his absences from New Harmony grew more frequent.

Maclure was also becoming thoroughly disenchanted with his partner, Robert Owen. He was impatient with Owen's ineffective organization of the community's social and economic affairs, and he felt that Madame Fretageot was coming too much under Owen's influence. He now began to realize that Owen's educational method was not identical to Pestalozzianism and in writing to Madame Fretageot called it a "parrot method"

Now you seem to prefer the parrot method of sticking incomprehensibles into the memories of Children as you would do pins in a pincushion, to the Pestalozzian System as taught by Mr. Neef, who I have reason to believe by experience has taught it in greater perfection than ever it was taught before. Neef, like all men, has his failing, but as a teacher he has made more clever men for the number he was allowed to educate than I believe ever came from any School on earth. This is not visionary theories of stars, spheres, &c., but positive and usefull practice.[19]

Although there were basic similarities in the educational views of Pestalozzi, Neef, Maclure, and Owen, subtle differences existed. Maclure, like other more recent interpreters, was first impressed by the similarities, and only later did he recognize the variations. Owen had developed his educational method at New Lanark quite independently of Pestalozzi. Owen's own sons attended Emmanuel Fellenberg's school at Hofwyl. In 1804, Pestalozzi and Fellenberg had attempted to operate a joint educational institute but were unable to cooperate. Maclure, who had visited both Fellenberg at Hofwyl and Pestalozzi at Yverdon, preferred the more permissive and egalitarian school of Pestalozzi.

In March 1827, Madame Fretageot wrote that she could no longer work with Neef, whom she described as "the most thoughtless creature that I know; if he had not his wife he would not have a penny and shirt for his use." She added that Maclure had overrated Neef's teaching abilities and claimed that his students were learning "vulgar manners" from him.[20] Apparently, the antagonism between the two teachers did not escape their students' notice. Madame Fretageot's students made up a song which they used to taunt Neef's students:

Number 2 pigs locked up in a pen,
When they get out, it's now and then;
When they get out, they sneak about,
For fear old Neef will find them out.[21]

Paul Brown's *Twelve Months in New Harmony* refers to attacks made on Neef's character and teaching method by an anonymous critic. Gerard Troost, a long-time friend of Neef, penned a public defense which asserted that Neef's students in his Pennsylvania schools were well educated, successful, and "more enlightened and unprejudiced than the generality of men." Although he acknowledged that Neef's unprejudiced mind and enlightened mode of teaching had made him many enemies, Troost declared:

I have been for seventeen years acquainted with J. Neef: I have found that every one whose mind was not blinded by fanaticism, who was not envious of the real merit which he possessed, was the friend of Neef.[22]

The Owen–Maclure Controversies   In the course of the New Harmony experiment, the basic differences which existed between the principal figures, Owen and Maclure, came to the surface. By the spring of 1827 the Owenite Community of Equality was on the verge of complete disintegration, as Owen and Maclure contested over financial and educational matters. Neither of the philanthropists had ever clearly specified their financial obligations. While Owen asserted that Maclure was a full partner, Maclure maintained that his liability extended to only one-half of Owen's losses up to a maximum of $10,000. Financial matters remained confused until Frederick Rapp, the agent for the former owners of New Harmony, came on May 1, 1827 to collect an installment of $20,000 which was due on the $40,000 still owed to the Rappites. While Owen insisted that Maclure was liable for $90,000, Maclure claimed that he owed Owen a maximum of $21,000, or $11,000 on the Education Society's lease and $10,000 as a forfeiture on his guarantee of Owen's losses.

Offering a compromise, Maclure agreed to pay $40,000 to the

Rappites if Owen agreed to give him a deed to the Education Society's property. Maclure paid Rapp and received bonds representing Owen's remaining indebtedness of $40,000. Maclure filed suit against Owen for the amount, and Owen filed a countersuit claiming that Maclure owed him $90,000. After some embarrassing litigation, two arbitrators arranged an out-of-court settlement which fixed Maclure's indebtedness to Owen at $5,000. This payment was made on May 3, 1827. Owen gave Maclure an unrestricted deed to 490 acres of New Harmony with the sum of $44,000 fixed as the consideration.[23] This financial controversy became a public matter which further weakened the community. Since the community had been originally organized on the premise of common ownership, it was ironic that so much effort was spent on litigation over property.

The essential differences between Owen and Maclure were not restricted to financial obligations but also extended into educational questions. At the community meeting of August 6, 1826, Owen had criticized the educators whom Maclure had brought to New Harmony. He charged them with failing to organize the schools properly despite their presence in the community for more than six months. Maclure's educators, he alleged, had also failed to prepare the students in communitarian principles. At meetings on August 6, 13, and 20, Owen proposed a new system of social education to achieve the desired communitarian indoctrination. The heart of Owen's proposal consisted of three weekly evening lectures to be attended by the entire community, children as well as adults. Lectures on various trades and occupations would replace the systematic instruction in mineralogy, chemistry, and mechanics. There was to be no distinction between teacher and student, and practical experience was the only requirement needed for lecturing. Visual aids, maps, and globes were to be used in teaching geography and other subjects.[24]

Owen's plans for social education undermined the educational efforts of Maclure and the Education Society. Owen had come under the influence of Lancasterian monitorial education in which a trained teacher would quickly instruct his students in a particular subject or skill. These hastily prepared monitors would then teach other students. At the time of the New Harmony experiment, monitorialism was very popular in the larger cities of the United States such as Philadelphia and New York, where it was used by proponents of massive but inexpensive education. As could be expected, the Pestalozzians, Maclure and Neef, opposed a system which relied largely on unprepared teachers. They could not accept a system which relied on haste rather than on the slow, thorough, and deliberate learning emphasized by Pestalozzi.

Owen's new plan of social education made the lecture the central phase of instruction. Owen was becoming increasingly obsessed with his own rhetoric as a means of social and educational reform. Maclure and Neef had always opposed the excessive concentration on verbalism. Maclure said that Owen was proposing a "parrot" method by which children would repeat words without understanding them. Such a step would be retrogressive rather than advancing Pestalozzi's progressive method of natural education.

Owen's plan of social education also minimized the importance of expertise in educational method and competence in subject matter. Neef, for example, was thoroughly prepared in Pestalozzian methodology. Say, Lesueur, Troost, and the other naturalists were competent scientists who engaged in careful research. Owen, in denying the importance of careful pedagogical and scientific training, asserted that practical experience was the only requirement for lecturing. In attempting to implement his plan of social education, Owen found that he still had to rely on the members of Maclure's Education Society for much of the instruction. Like many of Owen's proposals, the plan for social education was abandoned after only a few lectures. Nevertheless, the gulf between Owen and the Education Society had widened.

As a result of the confusing financial litigation between Owen and Maclure, the community entered the throes of complete disintegration. The relationship between the school and the community completely collapsed. When the Education Society requested payment for education on the basis of labor for labor, the Agricultural Society refused to render either goods, services, or money for the tuition of its children. The Mechanic's Society completely repudiated any obligation to the Education Society.

Neef's Reply to Owen's Farewell   By May of 1827 New Harmony had ceased to exist as a communitarian enterprise and most observers agreed that Owen's "Community of Equality" was dead. On May 26, 1827, Owen delivered his "farewell address" to the remaining residents and blamed the community's difficulties on the failure of Maclure's educational system. Owen specifically charged that Maclure's improper organization of the educational system had hampered the community's development. Further, he asserted that dissension among the members of the Education Society had impaired the school's effectiveness. In his attack on Maclure's educators, Owen insisted that a single, unified school system should have been created instead of a number of separate self-contained and competing schools. If the educational system had been organized properly, then all of the community's children would have been educated according to communitarian values. Owen continued his attack by stating:

If the schools had been in operation upon the very superior plan upon which I have been led to expect they would be, . . . it would have been . . . practicable, even with such materials, . . . to have succeeded in amalgamating the whole into a community.

You also know that the chief difficulty . . . arose from the differences of opinion among the professors and teachers brought here by Mr. Maclure, relative to the education of the children, and to the consequent delay in putting any of their system into operation.

Having been led to entertain very high expectations of . . . these individuals, I looked to them to establish superior arrangements for the instruction of all ages, and I was induced to suppose that the population would be compensated by the unequalled excellence of the system when put into operation; and in consequence of the unlimited confidence which I placed in these individuals to execute this most important part of my plan, . . . I have been disappointed. Instead of forming one well-digested arrangement, in which all the children . . . should have the benefit of the superior qualifications possessed by each professor and instructor, each principal teacher undertook the entire instruction of a certain number of pupils, by which arrangement they were prevented from associating with other pupils.

By this error ... the children were educated in different habits, dispositions, and feelings, when it was my most earnest desire that all the children should be educated in similar habits, dispositions, and feelings, and ... brought up truly as members of one large family, without a single discordant feeling.

It is true that each of the professors ... possessed considerable abilities in particular branches of education, but the union of the best qualities and qualifications of ... even the best modern teachers is required to form the character of the rising generation ... and enable children when they attain maturity to become sufficiently rational and intelligent to make good, useful members of the social system.[25]

Neef, like Owen, was preparing to leave the disintegrating community, but before departing he replied to Owen's attack on the Education Society. Neef, one of a group of "self-styled republicans," bluntly asserted that the community had failed because of Owen's incompetence. Richard Leopold, Robert Dale Owen's biographer, says that these "disgruntled democrats" came near to the truth. According to Leopold:

The New Harmony experiment was characterized by a total lack of a well thought out, consistent program, an inexcusable failure to regulate the quantity and quality of the participants, and absence of wise leadership, and a sheer inability to pay its own way. To be sure, Robert Owen's success as a manufacturer in Scotland was no indication that he could make American backwoodsmen proper exponents of communal life. His motives, despite contemporary slander, were of the highest.[26]

Neef had never really accepted Owen's leadership of the community and distrusted his philanthropism. In an earlier dispute over boundary lines, Neef had accused Owen of violating the charter which established the Education Society. He claimed that Owen really wanted to repossess the land and buildings which were supposedly the property of the Education Society. Neef, like Brown and others, believed that Owen should immediately surrender his ownership of New Harmony to the members of the community. When Owen refused, they questioned his motives as a genuine philanthropist.[27] In replying to Owen's address, Neef challenged his contention that the Education Society had improperly organized the schools. He asserted that the failure of the experiment was not the fault of any individual or group other than Owen, himself. Neef denied Owen's attack by asserting:

It is neither the superabundance of the "opposing habits and feelings of the mass of individuals collected at New Harmony, nor the undertaking of each principal teacher of the entire instruction of a certain number of pupils," to which we must look for the true cause of the miscarriage of your scheme. Your conduct, Sir, is the sole and only source of this abortion.[28]

In the last days of the New Harmony experiment, the participants hurled charges and countercharges at each other. Owen chronically reorganized the community, and no single plan had sufficient time to work effectively. Although dissension among the principal teachers certainly did not strengthen the experiment, Owen, himself, had interfered with the educational system by trying to introduce his ill-conceived plan of social education. Neef again blamed Owen for impairing the work of the schools:

All the individuals who came to New Harmony, had two objects in view. The first was to get rid of the inconveniences and miseries of the individual system; and the second, with those that had children, to have their children properly educated. Now, Sir, you have done everything in your power to thwart these two objects. Hence, your failure.[29]

It should be noted that Neef did not disagree with Owen's antagonism to private property and individual ownership. Neef, too, believed that it was possible to create a reformed society based on common property. While affirming his own commitment to the doctrine of economic and social equality, Neef did not believe that Owen's actual deeds had fulfilled his preachments against private ownership:

All your multifarious writings, speeches, lectures, addresses teem with denunciations against individual property, against competition, against inequality. Common property, co-operation, equality, form, according to your doctrines, the true and only basis of social happiness. Every man that has but one grain of common sense, must perceive that you are right, that your doctrine coincides with . . . experience: and had your practice and conduct been in concord with your professions, the social system, by this time, would be so solidly fixed at this place as the rock.[30]

Neef said that his arrival at New Harmony, on March 20, 1826, had been marred by the many discussions which occurred on the question of property valuations. This obsession with private property had impeded the formation of a genuine community of equality. To remedy this situation, Neef had proposed that Owen give the 2,500 acres of New Harmony land to the community members, or at least sell it to them for four dollars per acre. When Owen refused to yield his ownership, Neef began to question his philanthropic motivation. Neef also felt that the participants in the community would not work for the common good since their status would be uncertain as long as Owen possessed the community property:

To talk of common property, co-operation, of industry, economy, carefulness . . . to . . . people that did not own . . . the ground on which they lived, that were liable to be expelled every moment, that had no interest in being frugal, industrious, economical, or careful, was just as wise as if . . . southern planters should preach such doctrines to . . . black citizens. To make . . . human beings industrious, . . . you must make it their palpable interest to be so. But what interest had the people here to be industrious?[31]

Thus, Neef's participation in Owen's community ended on a sour note. The "Community of Equality" had failed to materialize, and the educational system had not worked. In 1828, Neef left New Harmony and went to Cincinnati where he tried to establish a school. Six years later, he returned to the Indiana village. He would later see two of his daughters wed to Owen's sons. Neef's descendants would also be Owen's. Before concluding this short biography of Neef, some evaluation might be made regarding the impact of the New Harmony experiment on the course of American education. Again, any judgment of Neef's particular contribution must be related to the larger social experiment.

The Educational Significance of New Harmony   Owen failed to create an Indiana utopia. By the time of his New Harmony experiment, Owen was unable to concentrate on any single matter: he was engaged in a variety of plans and programs but was unable to complete any of them. Owen's experiment was shortlived and lacked the communal cement needed to hold it together. Where such communities have succeeded in the United States, they have been sustained by religious commitments rather than by political or sociological doctrines.

Neef had accepted Owen's belief in man's basic equality, and he felt that property had produced social inequalities. Neef did not trust Owen's motives or abilities in establishing an equalitarian community, however. In all events, Neef was a secondary figure in the planning and theorizing that were involved in the social phase of the community. He was more important in the educational aspects of New Harmony which involved him in the organization, administration, and instruction of the higher school, the largest of the three schools in Maclure's educational system. Although this school used the Pestalozzian method, it also bore the imprint of Maclure's distinctive socioeconomic and educational philosophy.

Lockwood, who wrote the pioneer work on New Harmony in 1905, claimed that the community had achieved a number of significant educational contributions. It was, he said, the location of the first infant school, kindergarten, and trade school in the United States; the first free public school system in the United States; and a significant center for teacher education.[32] Since many more recent treatments of New Harmony have accepted Lockwood's assessment, it is possible to evaluate New Harmony's educational contribution in terms of this pioneer work.

New Harmony may well have been the location of the first infant school in the United States. Robert Owen, who established an infant school at New Lanark, was a pioneer proponent of early childhood education. He believed that very young children needed a special environment to expose them to socializing activities, stories and games, as well, as some intellectual experiences. Madame Fretageot was to have conducted such an infant school at New Harmony. Her decision to establish a general school as a rival to Neef's higher school destroyed any major concentration on early childhood education. Neef, himself, was not a major force in the short-lived infant school.

Lockwood's claim that New Harmony possessed the first kindergarten in the United States was exaggerated. The kindergarten was a particular type of early childhood institution developed by Friedrich Froebel, 1782–1852. Although there is overwhelming evidence that the educational theories of Fellenberg and Pestalozzi had an impact at New Harmony, there was no mention of Froebel, who had not yet developed his kindergarten theory of education. Froebel's kindergarten concepts were based on mystical Idealism, which both Maclure and Neef would have regarded as too abstract and transcendental.

Lockwood's assertion that New Harmony boasted the first trade and industrial school in the United States is better founded. Maclure was vitally interested in establishing such practical institutions in order to educate working-class children. Each student in Neef's higher school was to learn some trade or craft. Neef had a major role in planning the occupational instruction but the ideas for such training most likely originated with Maclure.

New Harmony's schools were public in that they were open to all the residents of the community. Although recognizing education as a vital component of the community, the Owenites did not develop a formula for school support. In fact, the members of the Agricultural and Mechanic's Society refused to pay for the education of their children. Owen and Maclure's socialistic experiment furnished little support for the common-school movement which Mann and Barnard advanced later in the nineteenth century. Lockwood's claim that the New Harmony schools offered equal coeducation is solidly based on evidence. They were probably in advance of most of the schools in the United

States on the matter of equal educational opportunity for members of both sexes.

Although many aspects of New Harmony's educational system were far in advance of most American schools, the community suffered from isolation. Although much was known and reported about Owen's social theories, little was known about the schools. The charges that the community was socialistic and antireligious prejudiced many against the experiment and blunted the possible impact of Pestalozzianism. It was not until the latter half of the nineteenth century that a more formal version of Pestalozzian object teaching gained popularity. It was the more socially respectable Edward Sheldon of the Oswego Normal School, rather than Neef, who was to be the great popularizer of Pestalozzian method in the United States.

Lockwood also asserted that New Harmony was a center for teacher preparation in the West. Men and women in the Ohio and Mississippi valleys who had been at New Harmony were supposed to have carried Neef's, Owen's, Pestalozzi's, and Maclure's theories into their own educational practices.[33] Such a claim is difficult to substantiate. Although some of the naturalists such as Say, Troost, and Leseuer continued their scientific research, they were not exactly teachers who had been trained at New Harmony. Neef and Maclure's attempt to popularize and disseminate Pestalozzianism suffered because not enough attention and energy was actually given to teacher preparation. Although both Neef and Maclure sometimes hinted at their intention of training teachers, they concentrated on disseminating the method by educating children. It was not until Sheldon incorporated a pale version of Pestalozzianism into his normal-school training program at Oswego that the method gained in popularity.

The greatest achievement of New Harmony was intellectual, in the broad sense, rather than pedagogical. Maclure did bring to New Harmony a number of scientists who made a distinct contribution to the natural sciences. After the failure of Owen's community, Maclure established a School of Industry at New Harmony, whose excellent printing press published the research done in the natural sciences. Such leading commentators as the pioneer author Lockwood, the intellectual and social historian Bestor, and the Indiana historian Wilson, agree that the intellectual migration to New Harmony was the most significant aspect of Owen's short-lived "Community of Equality."

The work of Owen, Neef, and Maclure should not be ignored by educational historians. In New Harmony's schools could be found evidence of the transference of the European educational philosophies of Pestalozzi and Fellenberg to the United States. Neef's, Owen's, and Maclure's emphasis on experience, activities, and interest strongly anticipated the progressive-education movement which gained influence in the United States during the early twentieth century. The views of Owen and Maclure also suggested the efforts of the social-reconstructionist educators who sought to use the school as an instrument of building a new society.

5

JOSEPH NEEF: EPILOGUE

The years after the disintegration of Owen's experiment were a postscript to Joseph Neef's career as an educator. His major achievements, disappointments, and educational experiments were over. After Owen's failure at New Harmony in 1828, Neef went to Cincinnati, where many of the refugees from the "Community of Equality" gathered, and planned to establish a Pestalozzian school. He corresponded with Benjamin Tappan, who had requested a prospectus of Neef's projected school. Although promising to recruit some students for Neef, Tappan feared that Cincinnati might not be the most desirable site for such an enterprise and proposed Steubenville, his own community, as a better location.[1] Neef apparently took Tappan's advice and moved to Steubenville. He established his school but it was not successful and left no permanent record.[2] Neef abandoned teaching and moved his family to a farm near Jeffersonville, Indiana, where they remained until 1834. Neef then returned to New Harmony, where he spent the remaining twenty years of his life.

William Maclure, Neef's friend and patron, had gone to Mexico for reasons of health. Despite his illness, Maclure maintained his strong interest in education and considered the possibility of establishing schools in Mexico. He encouraged Neef to join him, but Neef decided against it since he considered himself too old to learn Spanish. Neef preferred to remain in New Harmony, where he directed the work in the printing department

of Maclure's School of Industry, from 1835–1836.[3] On March
23, 1840, Maclure died at San Angel, near Mexico City.

In 1837, the famous triple wedding took place in New Harmony in which two of Neef's daughters married Robert Owen's
sons: David Dale Owen married Caro Neef, and Richard Dale
Owen married Anne Eliza Neef. Thus, the Neef line was joined
to the Owen family. William Owen and Mary Bolton were the
third couple in the wedding ceremony. A great ball was held
on the wedding evening and then the three couples drove off
to explore the Mammoth Cave in Kentucky. Neef's great granddaughter Caroline Dale Parke Snedeker, the granddaughter of
David Dale Owen and Caro Neef, called this a "geological wedding tour."[4]

Robert Owen's sons, David Dale and Richard Dale, are significant figures in American geological history. It is possible
that their association with William Maclure, the "Father of
American Geology," may have stimulated this interest. David
Dale Owen, who became the United States Geologist in 1839,
made New Harmony the headquarters of the U. S. Geological
Survey for seventeen years, until it was relocated in Washington. In his official capacity, he surveyed Wisconsin, Iowa, Kentucky, Arkansas, and Indiana. He later served as the state geologist for Kentucky, 1854–1857, Arkansas, 1857–1859, and
Indiana from 1859 until his death in 1860.

After assisting in his brother's geological work, Richard Dale
Owen became an instructor in a military school at Nashville,
Tennessee, and later served as a captain with the Sixteenth
U. S. Infantry in the Mexican War. During the Civil War, he
was stationed in Indianapolis as commandant of a camp for
Confederate prisoners. After retiring from the Army in 1864,
he was a professor of Natural Science at Indiana University in
Bloomington. From 1872 until 1874, Richard Dale Owen was
president of the newly established Purdue University.[5]

Neef retired in New Harmony, and drew an annuity from the
Maclure estate. On December 7, 1845, his wife, Eloisa, died,
at the age of sixty-two. After her death, Neef lived with his
daughter Caro and her husband, David Dale Owen. As Neef
advanced in age, the spent round which had lodged in his head

since the battle of Arcole in 1796 caused increasing irritation and affected his sight. It was during this time that David Dale Owen, a former student of the English artist Benjamin West, painted Neef's portrait. Although Neef objected that no one would want a painting of an ugly old man, his son-in-law did the portrait as the nearly blind Neef sat quietly for long periods of time. Caroline Dale Snedeker has remarked about this painting:

It was while he was sitting so that Owen quietly brought in his paints and began his portrait. It was quite finished before the old man knew what had been done. And there he sits now in my home with the patient listening look, his white hair thinly about his face, the bullet mark showing quite plainly near his eye—it is the best work that my Grandfather Owen ever did.[6]

During his remaining years, Neef was a familiar figure in New Harmony. Although perhaps over-romanticized, his great-granddaughter again furnishes a poetic description of Neef's twilight years in New Harmony:

. . . there under the trees he could be seen every evening watching the sunset. He was still able to perceive the light, and the beauty of the sunset colour was always a joy to him. He must have been a very quiet figure, standing there as motionless as the grey tree trunk beside him. I wonder what was in his heart then—all the memory of soldier marches, and charges, and journeys over seas, of eager studies and bold answers unafraid—all these were his, and yet at the end of them all he stood patiently taking like a child the few gentle pleasures that were left.[7]

After he had been bedfast for a week, death came for Joseph Neef in the spring of 1854, on April 8. After his death, Dr. Mann examined his head, as Neef had requested, and removed the ball. The irritating object which Neef had carried for fifty-eight years had lodged about a half an inch from the wound and rested on the palate of the mouth.

Joseph Neef, the soldier with Napoleon and teacher with Pestalozzi, was laid to rest in the Indiana soil of New Harmony's Maple Hill cemetery. He had lived for eighty-four years.

PART II

Joseph Neef's Educational Theory

6

JOSEPH NEEF AND EDUCATIONAL REFORM

In the early nineteenth century, Joseph Neef and Johann Heinrich Pestalozzi were active proponents of educational reform. They continued the struggle initiated earlier by Johann Amos Comenius, 1592–1670, and Jean Jacques Rousseau, 1712–1778, against formal education's excessive emphasis on verbalism, memorization, and doctrinal conformity.[1] Pestalozzi's pedagogical experiment at Burgdorf provided Neef with an alternative to traditionalism. Neef's school practices in Paris, Pennsylvania, and New Harmony, as well as his writings, consistently demonstrated his strong antagonism to what he regarded as artificial, unnatural, and repressive forms of education which ignored the child's nature.

Neef vigorously opposed inherited school practices deriving from that part of the western educational tradition which defined learning as the study of literary content, styles, forms, and categories. In this tradition, the educated man was a skillful linguist who had mastered the classical languages of Greek and Latin. Although emphasis on the classical languages had once been exciting and vital in the schools of the humanist educators of the Renaissance, it had grown increasingly sterile in the pedestrian hands of later classicists. In both European and American secondary schools such as the German gymnasium, French lycée, and English and American Latin grammar school, formal classical instruction had ignored the general intellectual stimulus of eighteenth and nineteenth century science. Further, such education ignored the social changes induced by commercial and political transformation. Although a skilled language teacher, Neef deprecated the value of foreign language instruction and particularly opposed the Greek and Latin classicalist's domination of formal education. He shared Pestalozzi's view that such "word-centered" education failed to prepare people for the realities of life and the economic demands of earning a livelihood.

The Protestant Reformation and Roman Catholic Counter Reformation had added still another dimension to formal education as schools came under the domination of various contending religious sects. Although Luther, Calvin, and other Protestant reformers advanced the cause of literacy by demanding that every man be educated sufficiently to read the Scriptures in his own language, the Reformation also fastened doctrinal conformity upon elementary and secondary schools. With the catechetical method, formal schooling degenerated into the rote memorization of religious and doctrinal texts by students. The secondary school's emphasis on Greek and Latin was reinforced by the Protestant reformers' admonitions that classical language study was still the most appropriate preparation for future leaders in the church. Since the Roman Catholic Church used Latin in its liturgy, Catholic educators were still committed to that language.

In addition to opposing excessively verbal and doctrinal education, such pedagogical reformers as Rousseau, Pestalozzi, and Neef also quarreled with the traditional conception of child psychology which ignored childhood as a special period of human growth and development. Calvinist educators held that man's inheritance of original sin made him naturally corrupt. Only those men predestined by God would merit salvation. Conceived in sin and born in corruption, the child's disposition was innately evil and required a constant and coercive discipline to exorcise this intrinsic human failing.[2] Since childish play and activities were regarded as deriving from the child's inherent wickedness, educators influenced by the doctrine of human depravity treated the child as a "miniature adult" and required that his behavior conform to desirable adult standards.

Although rejecting the notion of human depravity, Roman Catholic educators believed that man's inheritance of original sin had deprived him of bodily immortality and perfect control of appetite. Because of this spiritual deprivation, the child required an ordered learning environment where his intellect could be exercised and his will strengthened.[3]

Although theological differences existed between the Calvinist and Catholic bases for classroom discipline, both agreed that man was weak because of his fall from grace. In order to strengthen his will, the child required the discipline administered by adult teachers within the context of well-regulated classrooms. Unfortunately for the child attending the eighteenth and early nineteenth century school, regulation usually meant the generous application of corporal punishment by authoritarian teachers. Despite the earlier pleas of Comenius in the sixteenth century, schools remained dark, dreary, destitute "slaughter-houses of the mind" where children were kept rather than educated.

In contrast to the doctrines of human depravity" and "deprivation," Rousseau rejected the concept of original sin and held that man was naturally good. If there was evil, it derived from an artificial and unnatural society rather than from man's nature. As the least socially involved of all human beings, the child was naturally good, a "noble savage." Rousseau's *Emile* had presented a fictional plan for isolating the child from corruptive social influences so that his latent goodness could develop within a natural educational environment. Pestalozzi, inspired by Rousseau's romantic naturalism, had devised a method of natural education in order to regenerate man and raise him from the corrupt social state to a higher moral plane.

As an apprentice at Burgdorf, Neef had been exposed to Pestalozzian natural education and indirectly, through Pestalozzi, to Rousseau's romantic naturalism. Neef, a convinced rationalist, rejected much of Rousseau's romanticizing of the child as a "noble savage." However, he accepted Rousseau's concept of childhood as a special and necessary period of human development which exhibited patterns of growth and stages of readiness for learning. Like Pestalozzi, Neef sought to develop learning activities which were appropriate to the stages of child growth and development. In his *Sketch*, Neef promised to treat children as children; unnatural adult demands would never be placed on them in his schools.

Early Nineteenth Century Education In the traditional nineteenth century school, reading, taught in tedious fashion, was the children's chief preoccupation. The master pointed out one letter at a time and named it; the child repeated the letter until it was memorized. Words were studied letter by letter, and little attention was given to the comprehension or meaning of the content. The reading materials reflected the particular doctrines of the religious denomination which controlled the school. To ensure doctrinal conformity, children memorized Scriptural texts, psalms, and catechisms. In addition to reading, writing was learned by imitating the teacher's scrawl and reproducing it on a slate or in a copybook.

Since simultaneous group instruction was rarely used, each child stood, as if on trial, before the master's pulpitlike desk and recited his lesson. While one student recited, the others prepared their lessons in anticipation of their appearance. The children frequently became restless on the uncomfortable wooden benches. The child's natural desire for activity was considered as further evidence of his innate propensity to evil. In disciplining his charges, the school master often resorted to psychological and physical punishments such as ridicule, kneeling on pebbles or peas, sitting on the shame bench, standing in a pillory, or wearing a dunce cap. The rod, cane, and rawhide whip were standard apparatus in many early nineteenth century schools.

Pestalozzi and Neef, his disciple, struggled to overcome the barbaric school practices which were perpetrated upon the child. Neither theorist believed that effective education could take place in a fear-ridden environment.

The Pestalozzian Objection to "Book Knowledge" Neef agreed with Pestalozzi's epistemological premise that man's knowledge was based on sense impressions of concrete, physical objects. As sense realists, both theorists believed that observation or, sense perception, was the basis of instruction. Conventional educational patterns, they felt, had grown too abstract because of an exclusive reliance on verbal information contained in books. They regarded literary information as inferior to direct knowledge which came from observing real objects. Since the child lacked experience with much of the language contained in his lessons, he merely parroted these words back to the teacher. Like many of the later twentieth century progressive educators, Pestalozzi and Neef both believed that direct experience was a more effective way of learning than the indirect experience provided by books. Pestalozzi emphasized his rejection of verbalism when he wrote of the learning that he acquired by teaching poor children:

I learned from them—I must have been blind if I had not learned—to know the natural relation in which real knowledge stands to book knowledge. I learnt from them what a disadvantage this one-sided letter-knowledge and entire reliance on words (which are only sound and noise when there is nothing behind them) must be. I saw what a hindrance this may be to the real power of observation (*Anschauung*), and the firm conception of the objects that surround us.[4]

In rejecting an emphasis on literary education, Pestalozzi was critical of the classical Latin school which he had attended in Zurich. Neef, too, deprecated the value of language learning although he had studied the classics at the monastic school of Murbach. In deemphasizing language instruction, both Pestalozzi and Neef followed Rousseau, who had warned against prematurely introducing books to the child. Neef regarded an education based on literary symbols rather than on direct sensory experience to be detrimental in developing the child's reasoning powers. When Neef's students reminisced about their school days, they invariably remarked about the absence of books.

Although he was influenced by Pestalozzi's adoption of Rousseauean naturalism, Neef was also a careful student of the sensationalist epistemology developed by the French philosopher Condillac. Basically, Condillac held that human error resulted from the confused language with which man expressed his conceptions of reality. Although an abstraction merely named an aggregate of particular qualities or functions, men had come to mistake abstractions for that which existed empirically. When words were given a vague and unempirical meaning, the resulting confusion and error led to false information and to a distorted world view. Neef translated Condillac's *Logic* as an illustration of his teaching method. The following passage from Neef's translation provides further evidence of his distrust of words:

We observe nothing; we do not know how much we ought to observe; we judge in haste, without accounting to ourselves for the judgments we form, and we fancy we acquire knowledge by learning words, which are nothing but words.[5]

Neef's rejection of the highly verbal methods of instruction characteristic of nineteenth century schools was influenced by two sources: one, Rousseau's naturalism, which had been incorporated into Pestalozzian teaching methodology; two, Condillac's empiricism, which was part of the scientific legacy of the eighteenth century Enlightenment. Although commentators on Neef's educational theory have drawn attention to the Pestalozzian influence, most interpreters have not recognized the impact of Condillac's sensationalist epistemology.

The Pestalozzian Objection to Artificial Education   As educational reformers, Rousseau, Pestalozzi, and Neef shared an antipathy to what they regarded as the artificial content of conventional schooling. Rousseau believed that the twin pressures of verbalism and authoritarianism had repressed the child's natural emotions to fit the artificial patterns of a corrupt society. Paul Monroe, the pioneer American educational historian, clearly summarized Rousseau's opposition to artificial education when he wrote:

Rousseau formulated the new ideas in regard to social, family, and political reform, and finally in the *Emile* in regard to education. Education should not aim to instruct, but simply to allow natural tendencies to work out their natural results. Education should not aim to repress or to mold but to shield from artificial influences. Natural instincts and interests should control, close contact with nature should furnish the occasion and means of education.[6]

Inspired by Rousseau's romantic naturalism, Pestalozzi sought to develop a natural method of education which would, in his own words, "psychologize instruction." He, too, believed that a literary education artificially isolated the learner from political, social, and especially economic realities. Pestalozzi believed that each individual's possession of moral, intellectual, and physical powers had naturally provided him with the means of successfully and usefully participating in the real world. Unfortunately, the inherited patterns of literary education failed to develop these natural powers which were intrinsic to human nature.

In his schools at Neuhof, Stans, Burgdorf, and Yverdon, Pestalozzi sought to devise an educational method which would regenerate the poor. Such a method, he believed, would provide the skills and training which were needed for economic self-sufficiency. To popularize his educational theory, Pestalozzi resorted to the educational novel, which was a means also used by Rousseau. Emulating the example of *Emile*, Pestalozzi's educational novel, *Leonard and Gertrude*, depicted the moral, intellectual, and economic regeneration of the poverty-ridden Swiss peasants of the fictional village of Bonnal who had overcome their deprivation through the means of natural education. Anticipating the work of John Dewey in the twentieth century, Pestalozzi warned against an artificial system of education which divorced theory and practice:

Depend upon it, there is a wide difference between knowing and doing. He who is for carrying on his business by knowledge alone, had need, lest he forget how to act.[7]

Neef also opposed the traditional patterns of liberal education which supposedly exercised the intellectual powers but ignored practical and vocational preparation. Believing that instruction should be based on objects present in the child's environment, Neef held that such experiential object teaching would produce persons who were both rational men and competent workers. Neef conducted frequent field trips and nature study excursions which made it possible for his students to observe the agricultural and mechanical work being done in their vicinity. Neef's school at New Harmony included technical and vocational instruction.

William Maclure, Neef's patron and friend, believed that the artificial patterns of verbal and literary education were designed by the nonproducing upper classes to keep the working class in an inferior economic and political position.[8] Since artificial education left untouched the real economic concerns of the producing working class, they were ill-equipped to pursue genuine economic equality. Maclure's introduction of Pestalozzian teachers into the United States was motivated by his belief that this educational method would provide the working class with both scientific and practical knowledge.

Neef was also influenced by Condillac, who stressed the necessary relationship between theory and practice. In his *Logic*, the French sensationalist philosopher cautioned against relying on the exclusively theoretical, when he said:

To learn a mechanical art, it is not sufficient to conceive the theory thereof, we must acquire the practice of it, for theory is nothing but the knowledge of rules, and one is not a mechanician with that single knowledge; it is practice that makes the mechanician. This habit once acquired, the rules become useless; we need no longer think of them, and we do right, as it were, naturally.[9]

Condillac's emphasis on relating the theoretical and the practical had an impact on Neef. His students observed objects in order to discern their properties and the functioning of these properties in human social and economic activities. Neef did not deny the existence of bodies of knowledge which were valuable guides to man's conduct, but he did insist that such knowledge was properly acquired through the learner's direct experience. When based on experience, this knowledge would function in everyday life rather than being confined to the strictly abstractive and theoretical realm of literature.

As a convinced republican believer in economic, social, and political equality, Neef regarded Pestalozzianism as the most efficient educational means of securing an egalitarian society. This is why both he and Maclure were attracted to the "community of equality" which Robert Owen sought to establish at New Harmony. Although he never accepted the romantic sentimentalism of Rousseauean naturalism, Neef agreed with Pestalozzi that an exclusively literary or classical education bore little relationship to earning a living, raising a family, or participating in political decision-making. Like Condillac whose work he translated, like Pestalozzi whose educational method he imitated, and like Maclure whose guidance he followed, Neef rejected an education which claimed to develop the intellect by ignoring man's practical needs.

The Liberation of School Method   As a good Pestalozzian, Neef recognized that bookishness, excessive verbalism, and other pedagogical artificialities were serious weaknesses in the traditional school which needed remediation. However, the most serious vice perpetrated was the crippling of the child's mind, the repressing of his natural curiosity, and the dulling of his moral sensibilities by authoritarian teachers who secured discipline by enthusiastically applying the rod. While working with Pestalozzi at Burgdorf, Neef had witnessed the creation of a climate of love and emotional security as a necessary part of the school environment. Like the modern child psychologists, the Pestalozzians believed that the emotionally secure child learned more effectively than the anxiety-ridden, fearful child. Pestalozzi condemned the authoritarian teacher who deliberately created a school climate in which the child was governed by fear, punishment, and ridicule. In condemning authoritarian school practices, Pestalozzi wrote:

We leave children, up to their fifth year, in the full enjoyment of nature; we let every impression of nature work upon them; they feel their power; they already know full well the joy of unrestrained liberty and its charms. . . . And after they have enjoyed this happiness of sensuous life for five whole years, we make all nature round them vanish from before their eyes; tyrannically stop the delightful course of their unrestrained freedom, pen them up like sheep, whole flocks huddled together, in stinking rooms; pitilessly chain them for hours, days, weeks, months, years, to the contemplation of unattractive and monotonous letters (and, in contrast to their former condition), to a maddening course of life.[10]

Neef eagerly joined Pestalozzi's battle against the notion that children were naturally depraved, vicious, and willful, and in his *Sketch,* rejected the doctrine of child depravity. He recognized childhood as an appropriate stage of human development and accorded it dignity of its own. In sharp contrast to the authoritarianism which treated the child as a miniature adult, Neef said that as his pupils were children, they would "think, talk, and act childishly and puerilly," in order to "think, speak, and act manly" when they became men.[11]

Although living more than a hundred years earlier than such American progressive educators as William Heard Kilpatrick and Harold Rugg, Neef clearly anticipated the progressive doctrine of child permissiveness.[12] Neef, like the progressives, believed that children had a natural interest in their environment. Unfortunately, conventional schools and pedantic teachers often destroyed this native curiosity. Neef warned that the care of supposedly eminent teachers would cause the child's "desire of knowing" to "abate if it be not wholly annihilated!"[13]

As a teacher, Neef did not want his students to accept his words as unquestionable absolute truth but rather hoped to be challenged and disputed. In the tradition of the eighteenth century philosophes, rather than Rousseauean romanticism, he wanted his students to become rationalists who would muster evidence based on their own observations and not accept anything on the basis of someone else's word:

My pupils shall never believe what I tell them because I tell it to them, but because their own senses and understandings convince them that it is true.[14]

Above all, Neef hoped to create a classroom climate that was similar to the one that he had experienced as a teacher at Pestalozzi's school at Burgdorf. In his schools, he wrote the "grave, doctorial, magisterial, and dictatorial tone" would be absent. He would be a friend and guide to his students, their "school fellow, play fellow, and messmate."[15]

7

NEEF'S THEORY OF KNOWLEDGE

Joseph Neef's work as an educational reformer must be interpreted in terms of the sensationalist epistemology which was
embedded in his educational method. Like Rousseau and Pestalozzi, Neef had abandoned excessively literary or verbal
educational patterns and was convinced that all human knowledge derived from sense experience. While sharing a basic
empiricism with Rousseau and Pestalozzi, Neef rejected the
sentimental romantic naturalism which entered into their educational philosophies. He was much more attuned to the rationalism of the Enlightenment than was either Rousseau or
Pestalozzi.

Neef's life spanned the end of the eighteenth century and
the beginning of the nineteenth century, and he understood
the intellectual currents of the Enlightenment. Firmly believing
in the power of man's rationality, Neef sought to integrate scientific knowledge and empirical method into his educational
practice. By way of Condillac's sensationalism, Neef accepted
an essentially Lockean epistemology which asserted that human
knowledge was the product of sense experience. Neef can be
classified as a sense realist since he believed: one, in the existence of a real world of objects which were external to man; two,
man's sensory apparatus enabled him to acquire information,
sense data, of these objects; three, educational method should
follow the operations of sensation and enable man to form clear
concepts of the real world. A further examination of Neef's

sense realism requires a brief but necessary foray into the climate of opinion which characterized the Eighteenth Century Enlightenment.

Influence of the Enlightenment   The new world view which entered western thought with Newton construed the universe as a vast mechanism functioning according to its own intrinsic laws. When the eighteenth century philosophe spoke of nature, he most likely meant this all-pervasive, harmoniously functioning world machine. Through carefully constructed scientific experimentation and the accurate compilation of data, man could discern the universal pattern of natural operations and discover natural laws. While the greatest advances were in the physical sciences, the philosophes believed that if science was applied to human institutions society could be reconstructed in conformity with natural law.

Unfortunately, the dominant social institutions of the day were not in accord with natural law. Obsolete concepts of "divine right of kings" impeded the formation of republican government based on the social contract. Mercantilism blocked the free flow of commerce and violated the natural law of supply and demand. Artificial and archaic educational patterns based on scholasticism, dogmatism, and verbalism impeded the movement to a natural system of education. The residues of the old unnatural, unscientific, superstitious, ignorant, and unenlightened eras of the past thwarted human progress. Although the struggle had been inaugurated by Newton, Locke, Voltaire, Diderot, and Condillac in the eighteenth century, it remained for men such as Pestalozzi, Owen, Maclure, and Neef to continue the struggle to liberate men's minds in the nineteenth century.

With Rousseau and Pestalozzi, Neef rejected the idea that man was naturally depraved, a sinful and wounded, willful creature. Rather, man was good and, if corrupted, then the source of corruption was extrinsic unnatural social arrangements. To cooperate with his original state of benevolence, man's natural goodness had to be developed by a system of natural education, which would liberate his intelligence and bring about a moral regeneration. Rejecting epistemologies based on innate ideas or on Revelation, the theory of knowledge of nineteenth century educational reformers rested on sensation. From the misty seas of myriad sensations, man's trained senses could provide the data from which could be derived clear concepts conforming to reality.

Influence of Sense Realism John Locke's *Essay Concerning Human Understanding*, 1690, had worked an epistemological revolution which denied the latent presence of innate ideas in the mind.[1] Locke attacked the Platonic theory of reminiscence and held the mind to be a *tabula rasa*. Stressing an empiricist epistemology, Locke asserted that knowledge derived from sensory perceptions of objects. Man constructed his knowledge through combinations of simple ideas derived from sensation.

In France, Etienne Bonnot de Condillac, who was simultaneously priest and materialist, adopted Locke's empiricism, denied the presence of innate ideas in the mind, and asserted that sensation was the source of human knowledge. In developing a sensationalist psychology of learning which anticipated modern behaviorism, Condillac defined sensation as communication between the sensory organs and the brain. In asserting that Condillac exerted a greater influence on nineteenth century European naturalism than is commonly supposed, Isaiah Berlin said:

Condillac undertakes to reconstruct every human experience—the most complex and sophisticated thoughts or "movements of the soul," the most elaborate play of the imagination, the most subtle scientific speculation—out of "simple" ideas, that is, sensations classifiable as being given to one or the other of our normal senses, each of which can, as it were, be pin-pointed and assigned to its rightful place in the stream of sensations.[2]

In 1809, Joseph Neef published his translation of *The Logic of Condillac* as an "Illustration of the plan of education established at his school near Philadelphia." Neef had earlier mentioned Condillac's work in his *Sketch*. In 1817, William Maclure had expressed his satisfaction on hearing that Neef's teaching was following Condillac's epistemology. Maclure, who commented that Condillac was "the best I have yet seen," found the French sensationalist to be "free from those transcendental sounds which form entirely the German systems."[4]

Condillac's epistemology resembled Pestalozzi's theory of conceptualization and provided strong procedural clues which Neef used in constructing his educational methodology based on the object lesson. Although Condillac, Pestalozzi, and Neef might be classified variously as empiricists, sensationalists, or sense realists, of these the latter designation is most appropriate. All three theorists accepted the existence of a natural and objective reality which exhibited patterns or regularities, natural laws, which man could discover by carefully conducted observation. As stated by Condillac, "this design belongs to nature alone; nature began it without our participation in the design."[5] For Condillac, the mind was a feeling, or sensing substance which was comparable to the eye. Since the sight of the mind was like that of the body, Condillac held the efficient functioning of both depended upon exercise:

Indeed, an exercised mind discerns in a subject on which it meditates, a multitude of relations which are not generally perceived; just as the exercised eyes of a great painter, in a moment discovers in a landscape a multitude of things which we see with him, but of which, however, the pecularities escape our notice.[6]

Although man's sensory organs passively received data from physical objects, this passive sensation was inadequate to form accurate concepts. Condillac, Pestalozzi, and Neef shared a belief in the existence of a methodology of proper sensation. When sensations were acquired in an orderly manner by the process of analysis, the ideas which resulted were likewise orderly. However, if the sensations were acquired at random, then the resulting ideas would be disordered, inaccurate, and chaotic.

Condillac's treatment of proper sensation embodied five phases: one, man observed principal objects; two, he noted the relationships of these principal objects to each other; three, he observed the intervals that existed between these principal objects; four, he observed the secondary objects which occupied the intervals between the principal ones; five, he compared all of these. After these objects had been recognized as particular and discrete, and after their form and situation had been observed and compared, then a collective and simultaneous concept was formed.[7]

Condillac defined sensation as a way of analyzing an object by first mentally decomposing and then recomposing it. Analysis involved the successive observation of the qualities of an object in order to present them to the mind in the simultaneous order in which they existed in the object. Condillac's conception of analysis was similar to Pestalozzi's reductionism which held that proper sensation required that an object be reduced to its simplest elements or components. According to Neef and the other Pestalozzians, natural education began with the learner's direct sensory experience of objects found in the immediate environment. These objects were minutely studied in order to isolate their basic or essential qualities.

Pestalozzi and Neef shared Condillac's distrust of generalized, abstract, and wholistic conceptions of knowledge. Such generalizations, increasingly removed from direct sense experience, became clouded by error-producing abstractions. In their educational methodologies, Pestalozzi and Neef began all instruction with immediate sense impressions and avoided the premature introduction of abstract and verbalized definitions. Only after acquiring graduated and analytical series of sense impressions was the learner encouraged to form general classifications or definitions.

Neef's educational internship at Burgdorf acquainted him with Pestalozzi's concept of *Anschauung*, the mind's fundamental cognitive process. For Pestalozzi, concepts were based on sense impressions of external objects conveyed to the mind via the senses. *Anschauung* referred to every mental operation involved in conceptualization. Variously translated as sense impression, sense perception, or intuition, *Anschauung*, an all-purpose term, embraced the complex mental operations by which a person recognized the qualities of external objects. According to Curtis and Boultwood, Pestalozzi intended *Anschauung* to have a broad meaning:

Sometimes it is the process of reception by the mind of a sense-impression and the resultant production of an idea. . . . Sometimes it is the process of idea formation through a combination of sense-impression and observation—the latter term implying intellectual awareness or attention. Sometimes it is the immediate mental realization of an idea without the intervention of external things.[8]

Pestalozzi's emphasis on *Anschauung* led him to investigate sense impression as the necessary process in acquiring knowledge. He developed an instructional methodology which he called the "ABC of Anschauung," a set of graduated exercises of distinguishing, comparing, and classifying objects, by which the learner abstracted their essential qualities and formed clear concepts, or ideas.[9] Neef followed Pestalozzi's well-known number, form, and language exercises by which the learner was to recognize the number of objects, extract the form or structure of particular objects, and then name them.[10]

Neef's Orders of Knowledge   Following in the sensationalist tradition of Condillac and Pestalozzi, Neef held that man possessed a power, given the name of mind or of soul, which received and transformed sensations into ideas, which combined and compared ideas, and which communicated ideas through sounds and writing.[11] Neef distinguished four orders of human knowledge: one, that derived by man's own immediate feeling; two, that possessed through mental power; three, that deduced from analogy; and four, that acquired through the testimony and evidence of other men.[12] Although he distinguished four orders of human knowledge, all of these were the results of sensation. The accuracy of any idea, whether remembered, derived from analogy, or based on evidence rested ultimately upon the accuracy of the sensation upon which the idea was based.

According to Neef, the most reliable knowledge was grounded on real and immediate feeling. Using Condillac's definition of mind as a feeling substance, Neef asserted that only those truths based on feeling were candidates for absolute certitude. In equating sensing and feeling, Neef drew upon Condillac who had construed the mind's power as that of feeling the impressions or data conveyed to it through the senses.

For Neef, memory was the second order of human knowledge. Through immediate sensation, man knew only what he felt at a given moment. Through memory, man recalled earlier sensations. Often unreliable, memory was a less certain source of knowledge. To the degree that memory accurately recollected past sense experience, the knowledge based on this recall was accurate. Neef believed that appropriate educational exercises could improve and strengthen memory. In his *Sketch,* he indicated that he would exercise and improve his student's memories.[13]

Neef's third order of knowledge, analogy, was defined as conclusions drawn from known facts and applied to unknown objects. Although a fruitful source of knowledge, analogy, too, was subject to errors. Since it depended on the accuracy of memory, it was less certain than either primitive feelings or memory. In his discussion of analogy, Neef approximated what Pestalozzi had said in *How Gertrude Teaches Her Children:*

Knowledge gained by sense impression teaches me the properties of things that have not been brought to my sense impression, by their likeness to other objects that I have observed.[14]

Testimony and evidence constituted Neef's fourth order of knowledge. Of importance to man as a social being, testimony and evidence was the basis of history, tradition, and philsophy. It was a less reliable source of knowledge than analogy since its probability was relative and dependent upon the truth of human witnesses. Testimony could be distorted or falsified by the character of the witness and the inaccuracy of the reporting. Although he accepted testimony as a source of knowledge, Neef did not place a major reliance on it. He indicated that he would use it in his teaching only when other means proved insufficient and unsuccessful. Books, therefore, were to be the last source from which knowledge would be drawn.[15]

Conclusion   Neef was clearly influenced by the rationalism and empiricism which flowed from the eighteenth century Enlightenment. Like Pestalozzi, he distrusted verbal information as a source of knowledge. Influenced by Condillac's epistemology, Neef used sense experience as the essential strategy in his educational methodology. The following chapter will deal with Neef's attempt to structure the object lesson as a method designed to strengthen the learner's ability to use sense experience as the basis of conceptualization.

8

NEEF'S PESTALOZZIAN METHOD OF EDUCATION

Throughout his life, Neef claimed to be a faithful disciple of the Swiss educational reformer, Johann Heinrich Pestalozzi. Neef wrote his *Sketch of a Plan and Method of Education,* to acquaint Americans with the Pestalozzian educational method which he planned to use in his school at the Falls of the Schuylkill. Since educational historians have regarded him as an American Pestalozzian, an assessment of Neef's educational contribution requires an examination of his conception of Pestalozzianism. As indicated, Neef and Pestalozzi believed that sensation was the source of knowledge and of education. Both abhored the excessive verbalism and authoritarianism which characterized traditional schooling. Although a devoted Pestalozzian, Neef, like all disciples, emphasized certain aspects and neglected other phases of his master's method of natural education. This chapter will examine Neef's instructional method in light of Pestalozzianism and will analyze the object lesson which was his essential teaching strategy.

Neef accepted Pestalozzi's conception of human nature, which defined man as a being who possessed moral, intellectual, and physical powers. Both educators agreed that the function of natural education was to aid nature in developing these three germinal powers which were present in every man at birth. Since these powers did not develop simultaneously or harmoniously, the educator was to provide learning experiences needed to stimulate the harmonious growth and integration of these human potentialities. Frequently overemphasizing the intellectual, traditional schooling had neglected the three-fold development of these powers. Although some educators had erroneously construed the arts and sciences as the end of education, Neef regarded them as merely accessory instruments in bringing man's powers to maturity.[1]

Pestalozzi's Educational Method   Embracing many diverse theoretical elements, Pestalozzi developed an eclectic rather than a systematic educational philosophy. His educational methodology consisted of two interrelated phases: the General Method and the Special Method.[2] In contrast to the coercive repression of traditional schooling, the General Method involved the creation of a climate of emotional security. Like most modern psychologists, Pestalozzi believed that children learned more effectively in an environment which approximated the love and affection found in wholesome family relationships. The teacher who used the General Method was to create a learning situation which was free from fear and humiliation.

Once the emotional security required by the General Method had been established, then Pestalozzi's Special Method could be employed. The Special Method rested on two basic premises: one, since knowledge derived from sensation, instruction should begin with familiar objects found in the child's immediate environment; two, instruction should follow the gradual developmental unfoldings characteristic of the natural growth processes. According to these two premises, Pestalozzi developed his famous object lesson consisting of number, form, and language exercises. Instruction was to follow the well-known Pestalozzian strategies of: beginning with the near, the child's immediate environment, and moving to the far, or that which extended the environment; beginning with the known and slowly moving to the unknown; beginning with the simple and gradually proceeding to the more complex. The most important aspect of the Special Method was that instruction should begin with concrete, physical objects rather than with abstract language.

Neef's Adaptation of Pestalozzian Methodology Neef was with Pestalozzi at Burgdorf during the period when the Swiss educator developed his educational theory, and he was familiar with both the General and Special phases of method. Pestalozzi's emphasis on creating a climate of love and security was influenced by Rousseau's emotional romanticism. Since Neef was much more of a rationalist than a romanticist, he did not stress Pestalozzi's emphasis on benevolence or love. Pestalozzi had asserted that man's moral power derived from an interior and intrinsic germ of benevolence. Gertrude, the loving mother of Pestalozzi's novel *Leonard and Gertrude,* was the humane and benevolent teacher, who quickened and externalized the spark of love which was present in her children. This externalization of man's latent moral power had regenerated the villagers of Bonnal whom Pestalozzi had used in his fictional account of human regeneration worked through reformed educational practice. Through successive circles of love, the morally regenerated man moved from the immediate environment of home and family, to the community, and finally to the universe.

Neef was always a permissive teacher whose schools were noted for their freedom from corporal punishment, ridicule, and fear. In his *Sketch,* he made clear his intention of being a friend and guide to his students. His classroom conduct was generally much more liberal than that of the conventional nineteenth century American classroom. Like the twentieth century progressive educators, Neef believed that the child could exercise his intelligence more freely in an open environment rather than one in which inquiry was closed by fear and authoritarianism. Although Neef did not romanticize the child, he recognized childhood as a special period of human growth and development. Even Pestalozzi who claimed to have developed a completely practical educational method was too romantic for Neef, the hardheaded but not hardhearted rationalist.

To his credit, Neef did not completely lose the spirit of Pestalozzi's General Method, as did the English Pestalozzians, Charles and Elizabeth Mayo, and the later nineteenth century

American object lesson teachers trained by Edward Sheldon at the Oswego Normal School.[3] Neef was more permissive and less formal than the later nineteenth century claimants to Pestalozzian principles.

Although his acceptance of the General Method was somewhat qualified, Neef was always faithful to the Special Method's object lesson and to the graduated exercises based on number, form, and language. He never deviated from the gradualism of the Pestalozzian instructional strategy which cautioned the teacher, *festina lente,* to proceed slowly and gradually. Neef adapted the Pestalozzian object lesson into an eleven-step set of exercises which were designed to train students in the skills of careful observation, analysis, and reductionism. He indicated that his teaching would always begin with a concrete object and by analysis "descend from decomposition to decomposition till the whole subject is fully exhausted."[4] In designing his object lesson, Neef not only followed Pestalozzi's principles but also added ideas derived from his study of Condillac.

Neef's Object Lesson   The first step in Neef's object lesson involved studying the object as a whole.[5] An object would be presented to the students for their examination. After careful observation, the name was given and then the object was shown again to the students. Special attention was placed on the recognition of a complete object. Only after the student was familiar with the object was the name used.

Neef's second step was designed to give the students experience in determining the coherency, subordination, connection, and relation between two objects, or between the part and the whole of an object. To teach relationships, Neef used the example of the subordination of the hand to the body, or the leaf to the tree. For example, the leaf was part of the twig, twig of the branch, the branch of the trunk, the trunk of the tree, and the entire tree comprised all of these components. This second step followed Pestalozzi's method of beginning with an element, the simplest part of an object and gradually proceeding to the more complex part. It also followed Condillac's sensationalist epistemology of decomposing or analyzing an object by reducing it into parts. Emphasis was placed on analysis rather than on synthesis.

Neef's third step was an exercise in counting the number of elements, things, or objects involved in the particular lesson. For example, students would count the number of fingers on their hand. Neef was clearly following the Pestalozzian number exercise by beginning with the counting of concrete objects rather than with abstract numerical symbols.

Neef's fourth step involved the pointing out of the position or situation of an object. The intent of this step is illustrated by Neef's question, "Which is the position of the middle finger of your right hand?"[6] The recognition of the situation of objects was an important part of the method and frequently used in the field trips and nature excursions led by Neef. In his *Logic*, Condillac had discussed the recognition of principal objects, the subordination of secondary objects to principal ones, and the relationships between principal objects to each other and of principal objects to secondary objects. The emphasis on position or situation was a part of proper sensation.

The fifth step of the object lesson consisted in the pointing out of the qualities of the object. In asking his students to identify the qualities found in common objects such as snow, water, lead, or wood, Neef followed Pestalozzi's theory of conceptualization which held that objects possessed essential or necessary qualities and also contingent or accidental qualities. A basic aim of Pestalozzian sense instruction was to lead students to distinguish clearly between these qualities and to isolate the necessary qualities. From the isolation of the necessary qualities of an object, clear concepts result.

In the sixth step, Neef involved the learner in recognizing the shape or the form of an object. For example, students were asked to describe the form or shape of a table, a finger, or an arm. They were asked to identify objects that were spherical, cylindrical, triangular, circular, conic, or prismatic. Like Pestalozzi, Neef was attempting to involve his students in the concept of structure.

Neef's seventh step of the object lesson was designed to examine the different functions which organic bodies and their parts performed. The functions exercised by the sensory organs, such as the eyes, ears, mouth, tongue, and teeth were given particular attention. The functions performed by plants and their parts were also studied. Neef's emphasis on the functioning of man's sensory organs was intended to bring the students to a clear understanding of the relationship of these organs to sensation and conceptualization.

In the eighth step of the object lesson, Neef's students examined the uses man made of various objects. What effects were produced by instruments such as a hammer, pen, knife, and plough when applied to various objects? What uses did man make of iron, steel, coal, wood, or cotton? Neef's eighth step was designed to examine the practical consequences that certain objects and instruments had when man used them. In a rudimentary way, Neef was anticipating functional, or instrumental, instruction. Neef shared Pestalozzi's aim that education should be practical and should aid man in earning a living. At his first school, Neuhof, Pestalozzi had attempted to combine learning and industry. He always felt that a necessary phase in human regeneration was to give man the education which would enable him to satisfy his basic needs. William Maclure, Neef's patron in the United States, advocated an industrial education which functioned to advance the skill of the productive classes of workers and farmers. Neither Pestalozzi, Neef, nor Maclure had any use for purely speculative education.

Steps nine and ten were related in that the former was designed to make comparisons between various objects, and the latter to indicate the differences. In the final and eleventh step, Neef's students were to arrive at "plain, accurate, exact," and "precise" descriptions of any given object. A definition was a collective word which amalgamated all that had been observed, examined, investigated, analyzed, and determined in all the preceeding steps. These definitions were to be formed on the basis of sense experience and were to be the culmination of that experience.

Neef's object lesson was a crucial component of his educational method. He rejected highly verbalized, bookish instruction and insisted instead that students examine the objects found in their immediate environment, rather than memorize abstract definitions which lacked meaning in terms of their experience. The care which Neef gave to elaborating the Special Method revealed that he was more attuned to this aspect of Pestalozzianism than he was to the more emotional General Method. Even at this its earliest introduction to the United States, Neef contributed to formalizing Pestalozzianism. His interpretation of Pestalozzian philosophy of education was midway between the original version and the very formalized version used at Oswego later in the nineteenth century.

Neef as an Advocate of the Pestalozzian Instructional Strategy
Neef's greatest conformity to Pestalozzian educational methodology was his acceptance of Pestalozzi's Special Method. Neef affirmed his loyalty to Pestalozzi's instructional strategy when he said:

"Imitate nature," says the good Pestalozzi, "begin by what is simple, plain, known, by what you find in the child; dwell on each point till the learner is perfectly master of it; and never mix heterogeneous, known, and unknown matters." These precepts are sacred to me, and I shall always endeavor to keep them in mind.[7]

Neef fully accepted Pestalozzi's instructional strategy which used a series of exercises graduated according to the learner's stages of readiness. Neef recognized that childhood was crucial in determining the later course of human development. The skillful teacher was one who recognized when the child was ready for particular instruction and did not prematurely force nor retard the child's natural growth.

In his *Sketch*, Neef affirmed that his students would always set out from the "known and plain" and proceed with "slow speediness" to the "unknown and complicated."[8] This affirmation followed Pestalozzi's rule that instruction begin with objects located in the child's own environment. Accurate conceptualization also depended on the literal distance of the perceiver from the object. Pestalozzi had warned:

Never forget this physical nearness or distance has an immense effect in determining your positive opinions, conduct, duties, or even virtue.[9]

Instruction which moved from the known to the unknown also meant that the learner's progression in experience was to be unbroken. In studying geography, for example, the learner began with his immediate home environment before studying more distant regions such as oceans and continents. In his field trips, nature studies, and other excursions, Neef led his students from their immediate environment to adjacent but more distant regions. Eventually, according to the Pestalozzian theory, the student's experiences would be broadened to include the "widening circles of mankind," which led from the home, through the socioeconomic environment, to the world.

Condillac also stressed the development of reasoning from the known to the unknown. Every question supposed data in which the known and the unknown were intermingled. When the necessary data was present, it was expressed in such a manner as to disengage the unknown:

... if you want to make me conceive ideas which I have not, you must teach me by the ideas which I have. What I know is the beginning of everything I do not know, and of every thing which it is possible to learn; and if there is a method of giving me new knowledge, it can only be that method which has already given me some.[10]

Summary   Neef's basic method of instruction was distinctively Pestalozzian in that it emphasized sensation, rejected verbalism, used the object lesson, and consisted of graduated exercises. In his eleven step object lesson, Neef attempted to refine Pestalozzi's number, form, and language exercises into a more sophisticated teaching method. While Neef stressed Pestalozzi's Special Method of instruction, he did not accept emotional romanticization of the child which was present in the General Method. Nevertheless, Neef was a permissive teacher who sought to encourage his students' rational development.

Neef's object lesson was the primary means of instruction which he used to teach the skills and subject matter found in his curriculum. The following chapter will consider Neef's efforts to elaborate a curriculum designed to produce naturally educated citizens capable of living in a republic.

9

NEEF'S CURRICULUM

Joseph Neef wrote his *Sketch of a Plan and Method of Education*, 1808, as a guide to the students' program of studies in his school at the Falls of the Schuylkill. In addition to the elementary number, form, and language lessons prescribed by Pestalozzi, Neef also planned to offer the basic subjects of grammar, language, natural science, geography, mathematics, and physical education, which he believed were instrumental exercises in developing man's rationality. These subjects were not to be learned by memorizing bodies of literature but were to be directly experienced by the students as they explored the surrounding environment. In examining Neef's theory of curriculum, this chapter will consider: one, the adaptation of the Pestalozzian number, form, and language lessons to the context of Neef's own instructional program; two, the elaboration of a subject matter curriculum based upon Neef's conception of a rational education.

As a result of his educational apprenticeship at Burgdorf, Neef knew and followed Pestalozzi's special method of elementary education based on the elements of number, form, and language. Along with recognizing sensation as the source of knowledge, Pestalozzi regarded his ordering of instruction into the three basic components of number, form, and language as his greatest pedagogical achievement:

I also thought number, form, and language are, together, the elementary means of instruction, because the whole sum of the external properties of any object is comprised in its outline and its number, and brought home to my consciousness through language. It must then be an immutable law of the Art to start from and work within this threefold principle.[1]

According to Pestalozzi's three elementary means of instruction, accurate conceptualization resulted when the learner determined the number of objects present, extracted their form or outline, and named them. These Pestalozzian lessons were aimed at developing, establishing, and strengthening the skills of numbering, measuring, and speaking.

Number Pestalozzi had always insisted that natural education should begin with concrete objects rather than abstract ideas or mechanical rules. Pestalozzi's first stage in arithmetic instruction, the counting of concrete objects, differed from conventional teaching in the early nineteenth century which emphasized the memorization of abstract mathematical principles and the solving of overly complicated problems, such as the following example taken from a textbook, published in 1817:

If the posterity of Noah, which consisted of six persons at the flood, increased so as to double their number in 20 years, how many inhabitants were in the world two years before the death of Shem, who lived 502 years after the flood?
Ans. 201,326,586.[2]

Rather than the vague type of problem cited above, Neef used counting exercises in which the students grouped, separated, and compared concrete movable objects such as beans, stones, or marbles.[3] Both Pestalozzi and Neef believed that numbers had evolved as quantitative symbolic shortcuts in early man's original method of counting. They wanted their students to recapitulate this experience by counting concrete objects in the same way as did early man. The objects used in the counting exercises were varied deliberately so that the students would understand the quantitative relationships of more or less which

the numerical symbols signified.[4] Neef's counting exercises
followed the Pestalozzian strategy of having the learner manip-
ulate concrete objects until he understood the generalized
methods which systematized man's quantitative experience.
Neef's number exercises also used Pestalozzi's method of gradually moving from the concrete to the abstract. After the students were thoroughly competent in counting objects, they
were introduced to a series of "counting tables," consisting
of ten horizontal and ten vertical rows of rectangles which
represented the fingers. These tables were intermediary to the
introduction of numbers and were substituted for the real objects. Once the students clearly understood the meaning and
function of numbers, Neef introduced the basic mathematical
operations. As with all other instruction, mathematical skills
were gradually and thoroughly developed.

Form Carefully adhering to the Pestalozzian method of teaching form, Neef used exercises which were designed to develop
successively measuring, drawing, and writing skills. Measurement and drawing were intended to strengthen the child's ability to recognize and delineate accurately the shape of objects.
First, the students learned the proportions of various objects
by measuring and comparing their height and width, and drawing was introduced only after the students were able to take
accurate measurements.

Both Neef and Pestalozzi referred to drawing as the linear
definition of form by which an object's outline and surface were
accurately defined by complete measurement.[5] Beginning with
straight lines, the simplest element of form, the first drawing
exercises consisted of making horizontal lines, vertical lines,
and then right angles. The child gradually became familiar
with the basic geometrical forms used in drawing figures.[6]

Writing, the third stage in the Pestalozzian form lesson, was
introduced only after the students were competent in measuring
and drawing. Since they regarded the letters of the alphabet
as extremely intricate figures, both Neef and Pestalozzi believed
that children needed to practice drawing simple geometrical
figures, lines, angles, and triangles before learning to write.[7]

Pestalozzi warned that children who wrote before learning to draw developed a rigidity in the hand which destroyed the flexibility necessary for writing. More accurately, the drawing lessons exercised the small muscles of the hand which were used in writing. Neef also found that children were naturally interested in drawing, and he criticized the traditional school master's neglect of this skill.[8] Both Neef and Pestalozzi conceived of drawing as a utilitarian skill and regarded it as a means of stimulating the child's creative or aesthetic expression.

Once the students were able to reproduce competently the letters of the alphabet, Neef began instruction in writing which he defined as the expression of different sounds and articulations by means of conventional and convenient signs.[9] In teaching writing, Neef followed Pestalozzi's two part procedure: one, the letters, in strictly correct form, were placed before the child who studied and reproduced them; two, the child combined those letters which he could reproduce perfectly and formed words.[10]

Neef and Pestalozzi related the writing exercises to language learning, especially to reading, which connected the element of form to that of sound or language. Pestalozzi had prepared a series of reading exercises in which nouns, adverbs, verbs, and conjunctions were listed in separate columns. After the student had practiced writing these words, he combined them into his own sentences.[11] Neef regarded reading as a consequence of writing, and his *Sketch* indicated that his students would either write before learning to read or would do both simultaneously.[12] In *The Method of Instructing Children Rationally in the Arts of Writing and Reading,* Neef commented further on the relationship which he believed existed between writing and reading:

I perceived that reading consists in the utterance of the oral sounds, which are represented by the written letters; and that if I wish to instruct children in the art of writing thoughts, and reading them aloud, I must first make them acquainted with the elements of our oral language, and then with the signs or letters by which those who have preceded us in the formation and use of the language, had agreed to use as the representatives of those elements.[13]

Sound or Language Although he adopted Pestalozzi's de-
lineation of sound or language as the third elementary means
of instruction, Neef's method of language teaching was also
influenced by Condillac. Neef believed that men had developed
the power of speech, the means of making articulate sounds,
to communicate their ideas.[14] Like Condillac who held that
human conceptual activity arose from a combination of sensory
powers, Neef believed that speech necessarily depended on
training in accurate sensation. Conceptualization, and hence
language, depended upon the knower's careful observation,
examination, and minute analysis of objects.

In describing mental activity as a feeling, Condillac asserted
that man had used a "language of action" before developing
speech.[15] As a result of reflection, men verbalized this language
of activity and came to use spoken language as a means of sharing their feelings, either perceived or remembered, with other
men by using shared words. Gradually, the language of articulate sounds replaced the language of action as words signified
ideas which first had been demonstrated in the natural language
of action.[16] As a convinced follower of Condillac's ideology,
Neef believed that language, like ideas, was grounded on sensation.

Pestalozzi regarded speech as the means by which men made
their impressions unforgettable and their ideas clear. First, the
child became conscious of the qualities which he perceived in
an object. After recognizing the essential qualities of an object,
he used names or words to define its essence or nature. Verbal
definitions presupposed the existence of man's speech power
and the physiological maturation of the speech organs. As Pestalozzi observed:

Men first observed the striking differences in the objects that they
named. Then they came to name properties; and then to name the
differences in the actions and forces of objects. Much later the art
developed of making single words mean much, unity, plurality, size,
many or few, form and number, and at last to express clearly all variations and properties of an object, which were produced by changes
of time and place, by modifying the form and by joining words together.[17]

Pestalozzi had divided language instruction into three phases: one, sound teaching which trained the speech organs; two, word teaching about single objects; and three, language teaching by which men expressed themselves accurately about objects.[18]

While at Burgdorf, Neef had been Pestalozzi's teacher of foreign languages and his *Sketch* treated language instruction extensively. Following Pestalozzi's prescriptions on sound teaching, Neef's *Method of Instructing Children Rationally in the Arts of Writing and Reading* contained lists of sounds such as "ba, ba, ba, da, da, da, ma, ma, ma" which students were to repeat to exercise and perfect their speech powers. Like Pestalozzi, Neef had his students compile and learn word lists derived from natural history, geography, and human occupations.

Neef claimed that his method of teaching language rested on a solid grammatical foundation. However, his students would not use traditional grammars but would become grammarians as they deduced grammatical rules from their own language usage and wrote their own grammar books. Neef divided grammar into three areas: ideology, lexigraphy, and syntax. Ideology acquainted the students with speech materials derived from sensation; lexigraphy investigated and ascertained the different forms used in language; syntax treated the order in which ideas were expressed.[19]

Neef, like Noah Webster and others, believed that deliberate efforts were needed to reform the American usage of English. Webster, who believed that Americans should deliberately cultivate their national character, advocated a uniform national language as a primary instrument in achieving American nationalism.[20] Sharing Webster's enthusiasm for republicanizing American English, Neef believed that Americans as the "only sovereigns of a free nation on this globe" should use their republican government and inclinations to discard the obsolete linguistic residues of an "ignorant and barbarous" antiquity. In urging a republican revision of American English, Neef recommended the establishment of a special commission to study the American idiom and to create a new system of letters based on modern stenography.[21]

Neef also complained that the irregularity of American English posed many practical difficulties in learning the language. Many foreigners, he said, were deterred from studying and acquiring the language because of "numberless and almost insurmountable difficulties" caused by a "ridiculous alphabet" and the "incomprehensible use" made of it.[22] Although he had been one such foreigner, Neef had mastered English well enough to write his *Sketch* only three years after arriving in the United States.

Neef's Anticlassical Bias   As indicated earlier, Neef opposed the classicalist domination of secondary and higher education. In stating that he cared very little about what was called a liberal, learned, and classical education, Neef said that he preferred a "rational education" to the mastery of unnecessary and impractical ancient languages. He believed that devoting six to ten years in studying these languages wasted time that should be spent on more utilitarian subjects:

I cannot find the least necessity, nor consequently the least utility, in learning those learned languages. I am wholly unable to discover any real advantage which they bestow on the learner. I conclude, therefore, that it is repugnant to common sense, to lose so many years as is usual, in studying them.[23]

Neef's attack on the classical languages anticipated the reactions against Greek and Latin which arose later in the nineteenth century. In opposing the presence of classical languages in the curriculum on both logical and utilitarian grounds, Neef attacked the rationale usually offered by classicalists: one, Greek and Latin could not aid foreign travelers since they were no longer spoken; two, Latin and Greek words inadequately expressed modern inventions and discoveries; three, English classics provided better stylistic models than the classical writers.[24] Although finding no utilitarian justification for Latin and Greek, Neef yielded to the current educational fashion and agreed to offer these languages in his school at the Falls of the Schuylkill.

When he was the principal teacher at New Harmony, Neef again rejected Greek and Latin and was supported in this by

William Maclure, who shared his aversion to classical learning. Lockwood's pioneer interpretation of education at New
Harmony criticized Neef's anticlassical bias:

But in their eagerness to offer and do full justice to the utilities which
the New England schools ignored, Maclure and Neef eliminated the
cultures from the New Harmony course of study and made their
boasted curriculum as narrow as that which it came to conquer.[25]

Although Lockwood's commentary was written in 1905, almost eighty years after the New Harmony experiment, it revealed that the defenders of the classical languages and their
utilitarian critics were still engaged in the battle to control the
curriculum. Neef and Maclure were early advocates of a scientific and vocational curriculum. In 1855, Herbert Spencer
was still waging the war against the classical languages in his
famous essay entitled, "What Knowledge is of Most Worth?"
Spencer, like Neef and Maclure who preceded him, sought to
establish a curriculum rationale based upon the major activities
which constituted and sustained human life.[26] When the National Educational Association established its Committee of
Ten on Secondary School Studies in 1892, under the chair-
manship of Charles W. Eliot, this group again heard the arguments of the defenders and critics of classical education.[27] It
was not until the twentieth century that Greek disappeared
from the secondary school curriculum and Latin declined as
a major area of study.

Modern Foreign Languages   Although he had been the foreign
language instructor at Burgdorf and had demonstrated considerable ability in rapidly learning English, Neef considered
both ancient and modern foreign languages to be the least important part of the curriculum. Since a man could be rationally
educated without possessing the knowledge of a foreign language, Neef insisted that foreign language study should be
deferred until after the student had mastered his own vernacular. Although demeaning the importance of studying foreign
languages, Neef liberally sprinkled his writings with copious
Latin, Greek, French, and Italian quotations.

Although he thought foreign language study was unimportant, Neef yielded to public demand and offered French and Italian. He defined four basic operations as necessary in learning modern foreign languages: learning vocabulary; developing pronunciation skill; orthography; and phraseology, or using words in combination. Neef also anticipated the emphasis on foreign language instruction in the elementary school which arose in the 1950's. He held that it was easier for a young child to learn a foreign language than an older person. The child had only to learn the language while the adult had both to learn and unlearn.

Natural History   Both Pestalozzi and Neef believed that the natural environment provided the most effective means for teaching natural history, or natural science. Neef followed Pestalozzi's practice of conducting frequent nature-study excursions so that students could directly observe nature and collect plants, animals, minerals, and other specimens. Neef believed that children were naturally interested in nature. The good teacher, he felt, should cultivate this natural curiosity by giving full rein to the child's interests without the intrusion of dull lists of scientific nomenclature and classifications. Neef believed that nature, itself, provided excellent opportunities for the observation of natural objects which were an essential part of Pestalozzian pedagogy:

. . . we shall be exclusively occupied with finding out the various beings, which mother nature exhibits every where to our senses; and, after having minutely observed, and accurately examined any object whatever, we shall endeavor to describe it with plainness and exactness.[28]

Like Condillac, Neef believed that the first man was a natural observer who had studied both himself and the objects in his environment. Through the careful observation of natural phenomena, man had arrived at his knowledge of nature. It was through the observation of the regularities and patterns which nature exhibited that man, as a scientist, had discovered natural laws. Neef intended that his students would recapitulate the experience of early man in observing natural phenomena. In emulating the example of science, they would make new discoveries which would advance their knowledge of reality and further their growth in rationality.

Neef's democratic and permissive attitude were evident in his teaching of natural history. He planned to have his students classify themselves according to their own interests. Those with interests in minerals would become the school's mineralogists; those interested in vegetables the botonists; and those interested in animals the zoologists. At certain times, the entire class would pursue similar nature study, and at other times, individual students would follow their own special pursuits. Periodically the work of individual students and of the groups of mineralogists, botonists, and zoologists would be reported to the student body acting as a "committee of the whole."[29] Using group discussion, the students would classify the objects which they had collected on their field trips. Each student would have one vote in determining the proper classifications, and Neef said that although he was the teacher he, too, would have only one vote. After being classified, the plant and animal collection would be preserved in a cabinet of natural history.

Neef's method of natural history instruction was significant in two aspects: one, he followed Pestalozzi in taking nature study from the classroom into the natural environment; two, his integration of student government into nature study was more republican than Pestalozzi's paternalism. Neef's use of committees in which all the students worked together anticipated certain of the twentieth century progressive educators, such as William Heard Kilpatrick who emphasized the socialization occuring from cooperative group work. Neef's method of teaching natural science also was an early predecessor of the project method which Kilpatrick had popularized.[30] Neef's use of individualized instruction as each student pursued his own projects was very similar to the emphasis given to such study in the early 1960's.

Neef, who favored gardening as a learning activity, had his students establish a vegetable garden on the school grounds.

Pestalozzi had also used gardening as one of his favorite educational activities. Pestalozzi had originally hoped that his first school at Neuhof would be self-sufficient, and the cultivation of vegetables was to contribute to the support of this enterprise. Neef regarded gardening as a learning experience rather than a means of economic support. He planned to recruit an intelligent gardener as a resource person to give the students advice on the cultivation of their plants. Through their work in the school's garden, the students were expected to recognize the various reproductive and growth cycles of plant life.

William Maclure, Neef's patron in the United States, was keenly interested in establishing agricultural schools. In the early 1820's, he had purchased 10,000 acres near Alicante, Spain, for the establishment of a great agricultural school to be operated on Pestalozzian lines. Unfortunately for his project, the reactionary overthrow of the liberal Spanish government in 1823, forced Maclure to flee the country. Although discouraged by this abrupt cancellation of his plans, Maclure was still enthusiastic about establishing such institutions to educate the toiling masses for both economic and political independence. In his correspondence with Neef, Maclure discussed the possibilities of establishing agricultural schools in the United States. It was decided that Neef should concentrate on introducing Pestalozzianism and reserve the establishment of agricultural schools for another time. When he was not engaged in educational work, Neef attempted to farm, but he was not, apparently, a prosperous agriculturalist.

Like Maclure, Neef believed that natural science was a functional study rather than the mere amassing of inert information. Neef was aware of the transformations which early industrialization was working upon man's life. As an integral part of their study of natural science, Neef's students observed raw materials in the productive process before becoming finished products:

All the multifarious transformations which hemp, or flax-seed, for instance, undergoes till it appears in the form of a shirt, or napkin, shall be submitted to our observations; the seamstress, bleacher, weaver, spinster, hackeler, ploughman, shall by turns become our instructors.[31]

Geography and History   Neef's geography lessons, following Pestalozzi's rule of beginning with the learner's immediate environment, dealt with the location of the child's home and school in relation to the surrounding area. By means of field trips, the child was introduced to the concept of geographical distance. Pestalozzi had also used the neighborhood to teach geographical locations and relations. The children were first introduced to important places, then to the less significant, and finally to the names of these familiar places.[32]

Neef's use of the school environment as the point of origin in geographical studies followed the Pestalozzian instructional pattern of beginning very gradually and proceeding very slowly. Neef opposed the then current method of geography teaching which followed textbooks such as Jedidiah Morse's *Geography Made Easy*, 1800, or Nathaniel Dwight's *Geography*, 1795, in which collections of traveler's accounts, dry compendia of facts, were presented for the student's memorization.[33] For example, Dwight's *Geography* used the catechetical question and answer method:

Q. What are the animal productions of Poland?
A. Buffaloes, horses, wolves, boars, gluttons, lynxes, and deer. Besides these there is elk, which is said to be destroyed in the winter by flies who get into his ears and live upon his brain.[34]

Johnson also discusses *Adam's Geography*, 1818, which consisted of three parts: one, "Geographical Orthography" containing ten pages of the names of states, rivers, towns, for use in spelling lessons; two, "A Grammar of Geography," of fifty pages of major facts for memorization; three, "A Description of the Earth" for classroom reading.[35]

In contrast to these early nineteenth century writers of geography textbooks, Neef did not consider the recitation of the principal products, political institutions, or commercial relations of the various countries to be significant. As was true with most traditional forms of education, the conventional textbook approach ignored the learner's direct experience and emphasized meaningless words. Neef could see no purpose in having students memorize geographical facts which were easily obtainable in books.

Neef integrated the teaching of geography with the lessons on nature study, measuring, and drawing. In their lessons, Neef's students examined the surrounding countryside and noted the locations of gardens, fields, streams, and houses, carefully measured and plotted them, and then drew them to scale on paper. Rather than using prepared maps, the students learned map construction by making their own maps.[36]

The students were also to construct a large globe or sphere representing the earth, on which poles would be determined, the equator plotted, the hemispheres designated, and longitude and latitude indicated. They would then draw their own state of Pennsylvania on the globe, then the bordering states, and the farthest states until the entire United States was designated, along with its major cities, rivers, roads, lakes, and mountains. After they had carefully designated the United States, the students were to represent the neighboring nations, going from the nearest to the most distant, until they had filled in the entire western hemisphere. Finally, they would designate the oceans, seas, and other continents. Questions of longitude, latitude, scale, distance, and time zones would be considered as they arose.[37]

Neef, like Pestalozzi, was reluctant to include history as a formal subject matter in the curriculum. Believing it impossible for students to judge peoples and nations remote from them in time and space, Pestalozzi warned against teaching historical facts and interpretations to children who were unable to judge such matters.[38] Since historical accounts were evidential, they were far removed from direct sensation and subject to errors. Neef believed that historical study wasted too much time on obscure facts and events, and as in the case of foreign languages was unworthy of a major expenditure of time.

Physical Instruction Unlike many early nineteenth century educators, Neef included physical and military exercises in the program of instruction which he offered in his various schools. His emphasis on gymnastic and physical exercises anticipated the physical education programs found in the modern curriculum. Neef's views on the development of man's physical power rested on his basic definition of man. In accepting Pestalozzi's definition of man as a being who possessed moral, intellectual, and physical powers, Neef also agreed that these three basic human powers needed to be developed harmoniously and simultaneously through the means of natural education. In broadly defining physical education as the training of man's bodily, practical, and vocational skills, Pestalozzi regarded physical education as an instructional art of such significance that it could not be left to chance. Through his work at Burgdorf, Neef became familiar with the Pestalozzian system of graduated physical exercises.

Pestalozzi had devised an "ABC of Action" in which children practiced rudimentary movements and slowly moved to more complicated activities.[39] For example, the actions of striking, carrying, thrusting, throwing, pulling, turning, swinging were conceived of as the foundations of all possible human actions. Pestalozzi believed that physical education, graduated according to the child's growing powers, would produce the good health, strength, and posture needed for successfully pursuing any adult vocation.

Neef's physical education program rested on objectives which were very similar to those specified by Pestalozzi. He believed that graduated physical exercises supplemented the child's own natural propensity to activity. The proper setting for these activities was out-of-doors where fresh air and sunshine aided nature in producing healthy bodies. Like Pestalozzi, Neef believed that physical activities were immensely practical in preparing the child for his future vocation and in the art of self-defense.[40]

Neef did not believe that the lessons in physical education should become formalized, routine, or laborious. Believing these exercises to be means of liberating the child's natural energy, he regarded them as play and recreation rather than as toilsome work. He allowed his students the greatest possible freedom in this area and permitted them to run, jump, climb, and swim as much as they pleased. Neef enjoyed these activities himself, and participated in them along with his students.

Military Training Neef believed that physical instruction was basic to the self defense and military training necessary in the education of the free citizens of a republic. As a veteran of Napoleon's Italian campaign, the "old soldier" Neef gave more attention to military training than did Pestalozzi. Although Pestalozzi's pedagogical works did not provide any extensive discussion of military training, his students occasionally marched in military formation and practiced various drills. In fact, Neef conducted the military exercises performed by the students at Burgdorf.

When it came to military training, Neef was a complete realist. He admitted that some idealistic opponents might argue that military exercises had no legitimate place in a rational educational design. He countered by saying that such a naive conception stressed the world as it ought to be rather than as it was in reality. Drawing on his experiences in the Napoleonic wars, Neef claimed that his educational doctrines were designed for life in the real world.[41] Despite the sincere American desire for isolation from European machinations, Neef wrote that the United States was surrounded by hostile foreign powers seeking to destroy the republican example. Neef said that his American students were destined to become free citizens.

Must not those God-given sovereigns, always be afraid lest their subjects, comparing their own situation with ours, should grow a little doubtful of the truth of their political creed, and suspicious of the infallibility of their mighty teachers? And may they not in a capricious moment, think it their interest, to exterminate from the face of the earth every vestige, every trace of republicanism?[42]

Neef was familiar with the European policy of maintaining large standing armies and believed that permanent military establishments were pernicious to liberty. In rejecting the concept of a large standing army or navy for the United States he accepted the American ideal of the citizen soldier which he incorporated in his educational plan. Should European despots seek to destroy American republicanism, a nation of free citizen soldiers could form and repel any agressor in the name of their own self-defense:

> ... every freeman ought to be capable of acting efficaciously in the common defence of our country. I would peculiarly have a hundred thousand excellent rifle and marksmen, who, in case of a hostile invasion, from every bush, from behind every tree, from every ditch, would be skilled to send to certain death and unavoidable destruction into the ranks and columns of an invading foe.[43]

Neef was rather enthusiastic about military education and promised to train his students to be good commanders and soldiers. His company of students would be divided into squads, with the squad leader responsible for the training of the squad members. The students would execute different marches, movements, and tactics, first unarmed, and then, when proficient, with arms, a small firelock, bayonet, and cartridge box. They would also practice marksmenship, make entrenchments, and fortify positions. Neef indicated that severe military discipline would be introduced and a military code created. Although Neef believed in student self-government and classroom permissiveness, this freedom was not extended to military training where stringent discipline was to be enforced.[44]

Conclusion The curriculum outlined by Neef in his *Sketch of a Plan and Method of Education* was far different from the conventional elementary vernacular school's emphasis on reading, writing, and religion. It also was a radical departure from the secondary school's stress on Greek and Latin literature. Neef's curriculum was essentially a Pestalozzian program including form, number, and language lessons. The prominence given to natural science, geography and physical education was also quite compatible with Pestalozzian educational theory and practice. Neef's curriculum, however, was more than just a pale replication of Pestalozzi's own pedagogical plan. It contained points of emphasis that were uniquely Neef's.

Neef's curriculum proposed an education designed for future republican citizens. He encouraged critical thinking by his students while Pestalozzi was much more the paternalistic father figure who carefully guided his students. Since he felt that children must be prepared for adult life, Neef did not minimize the harsh realities of economic, social, or international life. While Pestalozzi was often sentimental, Neef was a firm rationalist.

Neef combined method and content in his curriculum. The object lesson was to be used as the preferred teaching method, but the students were to be involved in learning subject matters such as language, natural science, and geography. He did not deny the importance of subject matter content but rather sought to restructure the curriculum according to a rationale which: one, included functional and practical subjects and excluded ornamental ones; two, used experience rather than words as the primary means of learning.

The following chapter will deal with Neef's conception of ethical education. It was in this area that his differences with Pestalozzi were most evident and in which he made his greatest contribution to the Americanization of Pestalozzianism.

10

NEEF'S ETHICAL THEORY
OF EDUCATION

Although educational historians have frequently interpreted Joseph Neef as the lengthened shadow of Johann Heinrich Pestalozzi in America, Joseph Neef was an educational theorist in his own right.[1] While Pestalozzi awaited the coming of the benevolent monarch to inaugurate a natural educational system, Neef quickly adopted American frontier egalitarianism. He blended both Pestalozzian and republican principles and developed a theory of ethical education which was his most original pedagogical contribution. In examining his ethical theory, this chapter will analyze Neef's republican principles and illustrate areas of agreement with Pestalozzi.

Throughout their quest to develop an effective teaching method, both Pestalozzi and Neef believed that the education of the natural man was basically an ethical concern. Both educators believed that every man inherently possessed essential moral, intellectual and physical powers. A properly ordered natural education would secure the simultaneous and integrated development of these three potentialities. Pestalozzi believed that every man was endowed with the germinal moral power of benevolence or love, the source, means, and end of human development. This germinal power was to be stimulated and exercised within a proper educational environment of love and emotional security. In the ideal home environment, like that of the family of Leonard and Gertrude, the principal characters of his educational novel, children experienced love, especially mother love, and reacted by loving their parents. From the family circle, the child gradually extended his love outward to the community where he loved his fellow men. Through this humanistic affection, the child gradually came to love God, the Father of all. Within the moral sphere, Pestalozzi applied his basic pedagogical strategy of "going from the near to the far" when he said:

The germs of love, trust, and gratitude soon grow. The child knows his mother's step; he smiles at her shadow. He loves those who are like her; a creature like his mother is a good creature to him. He smiles at his mother's face, and at all human faces; he loves those who are dear to his mother. Whom his mother embraces, he embraces; whom his mother kisses, he kisses too. The germ of human love, of brotherly love, is developed in him.[2]

Although he believed that moral education originated in a loving home environment, Pestalozzi knew that the industrial revolution had weakened the home's primacy as an agent of moral education. In industrial society, the school assumed many of the educative functions formerly performed by parents. Pestalozzi's first educational efforts were with the poor children of Neuhof and the orphans of Stans. These children were the culturally deprived of early nineteenth century Switzerland, and Pestalozzi sought to educate them in the environment of affection and security they so desperately lacked.

Despite the presence of great similarities in the theories of Neef and Pestalozzi, subtle differences existed in the area of ethical education. Neef, a thorough rationalist, believed that a fixed moral order was inherent in the natural laws governing the universe. As a participant in a common and universal human nature, natural morality applied to every man. Renouncing any attempt to instill morality by preachment, Neef sought to stimulate his students to discover intuitively the natural moral truths inherent in their humanity. He believed that children could discover, understand, and practice the ethics which were rationally deducible from the universal moral law. In promising never to impose a dogmatic or authoritarian code of moral precepts, Neef anticipated that his students would become convinced rationalists.[3]

In contrast to Neef's rationalism, various interpreters have claimed that Pestalozzi's theory of ethical education was influenced by pietism, idealism, rationalism, humanism, and naturalism. Although his educational theory was an eclectic mixture of diverse philosophical strands, Pestalozzi was also familiar with eighteenth century rationalism and sought the moral principles which were intrinsic patterns in the universe. At the same time, Pestalozzi was also mystical and visionary. For him, man's moral power of love was really the core about which the physical and intellectual powers were to be integrated. The loving man would use his mind and his body in ethical pursuits.

Rousseau's romantic naturalism was a greater influence on Pestalozzi than it was on Neef. In *How Gertrude Teaches Her Children*, Pestalozzi attempted to describe Nature in rationalistic as well as romantic terms. Inconsistently, he described Nature analytically as a universal mechanism as did the eighteenth century philosophes and then, occasionally, lapsed into a poetic romanticization of Nature as the transcendent ground of all existence. Neef, in contrast, had little of the romanticist about him. Believing that children loved before they thought or acted, Pestalozzi approached the axiological dimension of education through moral sentiments of benevolence found in the good heart. On the other hand, Neef structured value education as a rationalistic framework and approached ethical issues through knowledge.

Susceptibility of Children to Moral Ideas   In stating the intention of exposing his students to ethical issues, Neef affirmed that, as with other instruction, ethical education would proceed gradually, step by step, with little initial abstractness or generality. In believing that children aged nine and ten were susceptible to moral ideas, Neef disagreed with Rousseau who held such teaching to be impossible. According to Rousseau:

It is impossible to form any idea of moral facts or social relations before the age of reason. Consequently the use of terms which express such ideas should as far as possible be avoided, for fear the child comes to attach to these words false ideas which cannot or will not be eradicated at a later time.

***

For my part I do not see any children more stupid than those who have been much reasoned with. Of all the human faculties, reason which may be said to be compounded of all the rest develops most slowly and with greatest difficulty. Yet it is reason that people want to use in the development of the first faculties. A reasonable man is the masterwork of a good education: and we actually pretend to be educating children by means of reason! That is beginning at the end. If children appreciated reason they would not need to be educated.[4]

No pragmatist, Neef rejected philosophers who claimed that morality was relative, had no fixed rules, and depended entirely on time and circumstances. He affirmed the existence of a universal moral order as an ethical basis for his system of value education and held that his system was "grounded on an immovable rock." Since man was a member of the moral order, Neef believed that he was capable of acquiring moral knowledge.[5] Although affirming the existence of a moral system in the universe, Neef's conception of value education rested on a natural morality rather than on a transcendental or theological system. In constructing his ethical framework for value education, Neef affirmed: one, the existence of a Creator; two, human life was sustained by the satisfaction of needs; three, human rights derived from natural needs; four, there exists a common human nature which is the basis of common human needs; five, men are dependent upon other men for the satisfaction of their needs; six, men possess personal rights and duties; seven, human rights subject each man to duties and to laws.[6]

Upon these seven moral premises, Neef fashioned his ethical lesson. Rather than asking children, as did most catechisms, "What is God?" Neef asked his pupils, "Do you have hands?" This and similar questions were designed to make each student conscious of his distinct personhood. Each person was in "exclusive possession of his own person, and a very considerable quantity of very fine, curious, and useful things" such as "eyes, ears, feet, a tongue, speech, a will," and a "memory."[7] After determining that each man possessed personal powers and properties, the students then considered the source, or origin, of these properties. Neef, believing that his students would accept the existence of the "almighty Creator" as this ultimate source said:

Him we shall call God, and it will very naturally occur to our investigating minds; that as we are intelligent beings; from Him we have received our intelligence; He is therefore the source, the fountain of intelligence. How infinitely intelligent must He then be Himself.[8]

Rather than a theistic conception in the Judeo-Christian sense of a personal Deity, Neef's view of God resembled the Deist's First Cause, a rational intelligence which had created man and universe. Neef was unclear about the method which his students would use to reason to the existence of God from a consideration of their personal powers and properties. Neef believed that God really and actually existed although man was unable to know Him. From the knowledge of their personal properties and of the great "unknown Donor," the students conducted further investigations and made new discoveries. Man's possession of a body and a mind subjected him to needs, and God gave man an "indisputable right to satisfy those wants."[9]

Since natural products satisfied man's need for food, Neef asserted that each man was entitled to share those products. Man could exert his physical and mental powers to satisfy his needs. In so doing, man encountered other beings like himself who owed their existence to the same Creator, experienced the same desires, and possessed the same rights. The Creator had endowed each man with the right of satisfying his needs without hindrance from other men. Since all men shared the same basic needs, they established society with its economic, political, and social means of satisfying mutual needs. In discussing the relationships of the individual to society, Neef asserted that human duties, laws, and institutions should conform to the principle, "Do Not Unto Others, That Which Thou Wouldst Not Have Done to Thee."[10]

Neef on Religious Education In their religious views, there were similarities but also shades of difference between Neef and Pestalozzi. Both men had some theological education: Pestalozzi had once studied for the ministry, and Neef had begun priestly studies. Rejecting ecclesiastical careers, both maintained an interest in religious matters and were occasionally involved in religious controversies. Deriving from a non-intellectual, undogmatic, emotional theology, Pestalozzi's concept of religion was a form of primitive, pietistical, Protestant Christianity, characterized as a "religion of the heart." Except for his frequent references to priests as "hypocrites," Neef's basic religious conception was unemotional as is demonstrated by his impersonal, logical, rational view of the diety. Though differing in their conceptions of the nature of God and the place of religious experience in human affairs, Neef and Pestalozzi shared similar views on religious education. They rejected dogma, doctrine, and the catechetical method of instruction. Neither believed that religious preachments resulted in forming a truly moral man.

Pestalozzi believed that feelings of love, trust, gratitude, and obedience had to develop in the individual man before being applied to God. Only by loving his fellow men and aiding in their perfection could each man come to know God:

I must love men, trust men, thank men, and obey men before I can aspire to love, thank, trust, and obey God. For who so loveth not his brother, whom he hath seen, how can he love God whom he hath not seen?[11]

In contrast to Neef's rationalist view, Pestalozzi's form of religious experience was humanistic, emotional, and opposed to the Deism of the Enlightenment.[12] Neef was much more in the climate of the Age of Reason, while Pestalozzi accepted and anticipated the nineteenth century romanticist renaissance. While Neef talked about reasoning to the existence of God, Pestalozzi said:

I know no other God but the God of my heart. By faith in the God of my heart only I feel a man. The God of my brain is an idol. I ruin myself by worshipping Him. The God of my heart is my God. I perfect myself in His love.[13]

Neef and Pestalozzi agreed that ethical education should stress morality without injecting dogmatic indoctrination. Several times during his teaching career in the United States, Neef was charged with atheistically corrupting the morals of youth. In his schools at the Falls of the Schuylkill and at Village Green, he was opposed as an atheist. The entire educational experiment at New Harmony was attacked as a source of irreligion. In his *Sketch*, Neef said that all religious systems were composed of two parts: dogma and morals. His school would not engage in doctrinal controversy but would teach the common morality which undergirded all religions. He expected to have students of different religious denominations. Since their parents would want them instructed in their own particular dogmas, Neef promised an impartial noninterference in matters of religious doctrine.[14]

Despite their doctrinal and ritualistic differences, Neef believed that all religious sects reflected the common morality which was universal to men everywhere. Since all religious denominations looked "upon a good, useful, beneficent, virtuous man, as an ornament to society," Neef intended to explore the ethical dimension of education from the perspective of the universal morality which undergirded all life and societies.[15] Thus, a common ethical system would be available without necessitating doctrinal intervention.

In some ways, Neef anticipated the compromise attending teaching of a "common Christianity" in the later nineteenth century common school. His view of a common, natural morality evident to rational men, exceeded, however, the compromise of a "common Christianity" which came to mean a nondenominational, nonsectarian Protestantism. Neef's ethical teaching exceeded the boundaries of Protestant and Catholic Christianity and included eastern and oriental religious and ethical systems. Like his intellectual predecessors, the eighteenth century philosophes, Neef believed that the various ethical codes, part of the great world religions, actually expressed and reflected a natural morality common to all men because of their rational nature.

Opposition of Catechetical Instruction   Since both Neef and Pestalozzi opposed exclusively verbal instruction and dogmatic indoctrination, they also opposed the then prevalent practice of catechetical instruction. During the late eighteenth and early nineteenth centuries, elementary vernacular schools were usually conducted under denominational auspices. For example, the New England district schools indoctrinated their students in religious dogma. In these schools, the memorization of the catechism formed a major part of instruction. Presbyterians, Lutherans, Baptists, and Roman Catholics, as well as other denominations, each had their own catechism, which was studied and memorized by the young members of the denomination. The catechetical approach involved the memorization of questions and answers, each of which contained a religious principle. While the recitation of the memorized response gave the external appearance of religious conformity and commitment, the anticipation was that with maturity the student would eventually internalize the rote formulae into religious practice and ethical behavior. A major rationale for the catechetical method was that this prepared the child to defend his faith against antagonists in other religions and unbelievers.

For example, *The Westminster Assembly's Shorter Catechism* was widely read in the United States in the seventeenth and eighteenth centuries. Although later catechisms were produced, the basic learning strategy remained the same. *The Shorter Catechism* contained 107 questions and answers which the children were to memorize.[16] In the schools and churches, public programs were presented in which children were catechized before their proud parents. The following excerpts from *The Shorter Catechism* illustrate this approach, which both Neef and Pestalozzi abhorred:

Q. What is the chief End of Man?
A. Man's chief End is to Glorify God, and to Enjoy Him forever.

Q. What Rule hath God given to direct us how we may glorify and enjoy Him?

A. The Word of God which is contained in the Scriptures of the Old and New Testament, is the only Rule to direct us how we may glorify and enjoy Him.[17]

In his fictional account of the school in *Leonard and Gertrude*, Pestalozzi argued against "mouth religion." Like Gertrude, the good village pastor educated by example rather than preaching. He no longer permitted his children to learn dogma by rote since this method had divided Christians against one another. In rejecting the old "mouth religion of the past," the pastor did not invent a new "mouth religion" to replace the old but prepared the children for a "peaceful and laborious" vocational life. He habituated them to a wise mode of life, the "quiet and silent" worship of God, and "pure, active, and silent benevolence to man." According to Pestalozzi:

The pastor based every word of his brief instructions in religion upon the doings and omissions of the children, their circumstances and duties in life; so that, when he talked with them of God and eternity, he seemed to be speaking of father and mother, of house and home— of things closely connected with this world.[18]

Pestalozzi's rejection of the catechetical method involved him in controversy in the lower-class school at Burgdorf where the working-class parents demanded his dismissal. Neef also experienced opposition to his common, natural ethical system. Condemning the catechetical method as a repressive system which forced the child to memorize both question and answer in a "parrot-like" response, Neef believed the student would understand neither question nor answer.[19]

Civic Education   Neef and Pestalozzi also differed in their ideas of man's relationship to the state and to society. As a convinced republican, Neef eagerly accepted both the American and French revolutions. He spoke of his school as a self-governing, constitutional republic where each student would have one vote in group decisions. Neef, the teacher, announced that he, too, would be limited to only one vote. Pestalozzi, on the other hand, applied his theory of paternalistic benevolence to political and civic life. As the home circle was governed by loving parents, the larger social context also would be ruled by benevolent governors. For a time, Pestalozzi subscribed to "enlightened despotism" as a means of initiating educational and humanitarian reforms. When "enlightened despots" failed to inaugurate reforms, Pestalozzi hopefully supported the French Revolution and the Helvetian Republic inaugurated under French auspices. Later, however, Pestalozzi recoiled from Jacobinism and what he considered to be the excesses of the headless mass. In his schools, he did not initiate student self-government but rather was "Papa Pestalozzi," the benevolent father figure.

Believing that the welfare of all classes was interdependent, Pestalozzi's citizenship education stressed moral values and vocational training designed to produce useful community members.[20] Feeling no strong class antagonisms, Pestalozzi believed that the general welfare, happiness, and prosperity could be secured only within the context of the spirit of industry. Pestalozzi's mother figure, Gertrude, spoke to Leonard, her husband, about the patience of the poor with their economic condition:

. . . God helps the poor man in secret, and gives him strength and understanding to bear, and to suffer, and to endure, what appears almost incredible. And, when it is once gone through with an approving conscience, Leonard, then it brings happiness, indeed; greater than anyone can know, who has had no occasion to practice self-denial.[21]

Although closely identified with Pestalozzi's pedagogical principles, Neef subscribed to William Maclure's socioeconomic views, which saw the upper and lower classes locked in conflict as the producing workers and farmers were exploited by the nonproducing upper classes.[22] While at New Harmony, Neef joined a group of self-styled republicans who constantly opposed what they considered the despotism of Robert Owen. In his views on citizenship, Neef adapted quickly to the egalitarianism of the Indiana and Kentucky frontier and proudly called himself a "backwoodsman" who had little use for class distinctions, aristocrats, and slavery.

Neef's model for educating the good citizen was the self-governing, naturally educated, republican citizen. Neef's values were those that related to man's social obligations, and he construed the ethical situation in the context of the effects and consequences which actions had upon oneself and others. He claimed to base his moral system on the uncontrovertible fact that every feeling creature sought to avoid harm. By reasoning, men could discern the patterns of natural morality which functioned in the universe. Neef said that his students would not passively accept all that they were told but would formulate their own beliefs and values.

Neef did not believe that children should be sheltered from the fact that social evils existed. In preparing for their adult social role, children should be acquainted with the dangers that would surround them in life. To avoid social and financial disaster, children ought to know that there were "cheats, deceivers, and imposters of every kind and description."[23] Nor did Neef believe that the good life prevented men from enjoying the world because of some theoretical, theological, or metaphysical system. His students would not "exert their reason upon chimerical conjectures or in building idle systems."[24]

Neef outlined in his *Sketch* and attempted to execute a plan for a self-governed school republic at the Falls of the Schuylkill and New Harmony. The constitution of Neef's school republic was to begin with a first statute reading: "Do unto others, that which thou wouldst have done to thee." The constitution would specify both inalienable rights and immutable duties, with duties being deduced from the rights. All other laws, of which there would be few, were to be only corollaries and explanations of the first statute. With the establishing of a constitutional authority in the school, the teacher's exclusive control of discipline would diminish. Neef planned to address his students on self-government with the following words:

. . . you are worthy to be governed by your own laws, or rather by the dictates of universal reason, which the Almighty has made a constituent part of your nature, and which you have now discovered; you are no longer my subjects, but you are, and must ever be subject to your duties. To be a member of your society, a citizen of your little republic, is my ambition.[25]

Based on the political system of his adopted nation, Neef's school republic would also have legislative, judicial, and executive branches of government. The student body would constitute the legislature from which would be derived the executive power and the court of justice. The students would have their own police power. Any student accused of violating the school's constitution would enjoy the liberty of defending himself against his accuser. If the jury of peers, fellow students, found the accused not guilty, then the accuser was liable to suffer the punishment which the accused would have suffered if convicted.[26] Far exceeding Pestalozzi's paternalistic school family, Neef and his school republic might have been comfortable among the most enthusiastic twentieth century, child-centered progressive educators. Although optimistic about the possibilities for a self-governing school republic, he must have been sorely disappointed at the failure of Robert Owen's self-governing utopian community on the banks of the Wabash.

Student-Teacher Relationship   When reduced to its essential base, the ethical dimension in education rested on the relationship which existed between student and teacher. Both Pestalozzi and Neef rejected the authoritarian concept of this relationship which construed the teacher as an absolute classroom tyrant and of the student as a subject prone to willful and disorderly inclinations. Both educators gave a greater rein to the child's interests and curiosity. Both recognized childhood as a unique stage of human growth and development and advocated a classroom atmosphere which was much more permissive than the traditional school of their times.

As already indicated, Neef, as a rationalist and a republican, believed that children were reasoning beings who were amenable to rational arguments. His constitutional and legalistic school republic was a proper institution for students to cultivate their basic and inherent rationality through the practice of self-government.

Although sharing many of the ideas of eighteenth century rationalism, Pestalozzi was also influenced by romanticism. For him, nature was not only an efficiently functioning mechanism but was also primeval, vague, and misty. Pestalozzi's ethical system rested on the feelings of benevolence which he believed were inherent in human nature. The pupil's motivation to learning came from love rather than fear. Love for the child would kindle love in the child, and from love would follow the sense of duty and obligation. Writing in *Christopher and Elizabeth,* Pestalozzi said:

... the schoolmaster should, at least, be an open-hearted, cheerful, affectionate, and kind man, who would be as a father to the children; a man made on purpose to open children's hearts, and their mouths, and to draw forth their understandings, as it were, from the hindermost corner.[27]

Neef wanted his students to think critically, to question, and to probe. He believed that unethical elements entered into educational practices when the student knew that the teacher was wrong but was not permitted to question or challenge him. In centering all authority on the teacher's words, even when in error, the traditional school had produced hypocrites among the students. In the traditional school, unquestioning and accepting behavior was rewarded while critical thinking was punished.[28]

Conclusion Neef was more than the lengthened shadow of Pestalozzi in America, more than a mere imitator. He contributed to the Americanization of Pestalozzian education. Neef's rationalism was clearly evident in the ethical dimension of education where it overshadowed Pestalozzi's paternalism and romantic sentimentality. Neef's ethical system was derived from humanistic and secular values rather than from religious orthodoxy. Neef's basic commitment to republican principles further contributed to his development of a system of ethical education which fitted the American environment. As it tended to do with all transplanted ideas and institutions, the frontier may have altered Pestalozzianism to give it a particularly American dimension. If so, then Joseph Neef was one of the instruments in this transformation.

11

NEEF'S SIGNIFICANCE
IN EDUCATIONAL HISTORY

Recent histories of education have relied on Will S. Monroe's interpretation of Joseph Neef's contribution to American education. According to Monroe, Neef was the first to introduce Pestalozzianism into the United States. His *Sketch of a Plan and Method of Education* was the first comprehensive treatment of Pestalozzianism and the first strictly pedagogical work to appear in English in the United States.[1] Despite these achievements, Monroe indicates that Neef's impact was blunted. In the development of American education, Neef's work was premature since it was too far ahead of the common-school movement. His teaching method failed to take hold in any given locality since Neef moved his schools too frequently. Finally, Monroe claims that Neef did not prepare teachers who might have diffused and perpetuated his educational theory and practice.[2]

An examination of several recently published histories of American education reveals their authors' acceptance of Monroe's judgment on Neef's contribution to American education. While most of these historians of education find Neef's attempt to popularize Pestalozzianism an interesting episode, they also concur that his impact was slight. Although Edwards and Richey indicate that Neef's *Sketch* was an excellent treatise on Pestalozzian pedagogy, they assert that residues of the New England educational tradition and enthusiasm for monitorialism overshadowed the attempt to introduce Pestalozzianism:

At the time, interest in education was at a low ebb. New England was more or less content to bask in the glory of the educational attainments of earlier generations, and the remainder of the country, without even a tradition of good schools, was in the first flush of excitement over the marching-club, mechanical, mass-production methods of the monitorial system.[3]

William M. French shares the view of Edwards and Richey, and he writes that Neef's two books on Pestalozzian principles had no great influence on American schools, "which were scarcely ready in the early 1800's for reform. By the time the schools were ready, the books were forgotten."[4] Adolphe Meyer finds the interest in Neef's work to be more antiquarian in nature than based on any major impact Neef may have exerted. According to Meyer:

. . . Joseph Neef, a soldier once in the service of Napoleon and later, for the better one hopes, a teacher in one of Pestalozzi's schools, translated himself to the United States. For a time Neef schoolmastered in Philadelphia and in the Middle West, with occasional flings at writing. Though his influence, on the whole, was of no consequence, his books on educational theory and practice . . . have been honored by memorists as the first of such treatises in English to be published in America.[5]

Although the educational historians have tended to minimize Neef's impact on the development of American educational theories and institutions, a number of social and intellectual historians have devoted more attention to his work. In doing so, however, these historians have usually treated Neef in terms of his participation in Robert Owen's New Harmony experiment. Lockwood's *New Harmony Movement* devotes a long chapter to education in Owen's community.[6] Bestor's *Backwoods Utopias* contains a well-written and thoroughly documented description of educational allies of communitarianism.[7] Neef is mentioned as one of the associates of William Maclure who tried to use Pestalozzianism as a means for social and economic reconstruction.

In terms of the New Harmony experiment, Neef was a figure of some consequence, although secondary to both Owen and

Maclure. Although the works of Monroe and Lockwood in the first decade of the twentieth century treated the New Harmony movement, educational historians have neglected this attempt to use Pestalozzian pedagogy as an instrument of social engineering. When the educational work of Owen, Maclure, and Neef has received serious study and interpretation by educational historians, Neef's role in American education will undoubtedly be reevaluated. If education is conceived of in the rather limited sense of schooling, then Monroe's judgment of Neef may still be adequate. If education is considered in terms of its broader social, cultural, political, and economic consequences, then Neef's work should be reassessed.

Neef as Educational Philosopher   Although he disliked the abstract, the transcendental, and the generalized, a reinterpretation of Neef's significance should offer commentary on his contribution to the philosophy of education. Despite his obvious concern with actual school practice and instruction, Neef's educational method rested on a systematic world view. A sense realist, he believed in the existence of an objective order of reality. Since man acquired his knowledge of this world of objects through sensory processes, Neef incorporated the empiricist, or sensationalist, epistemology into his educational method. Neef was not only concerned with methodology but also emphasized the axiological dimension of education. He consciously incorporated rationalist, republican, and secular values into his teaching and into the milieu of his schools.

Like most philosophers and theorists, Neef did not originate all of his philosophic premises. He drew heavily on the educational philosophy of Pestalozzi, whose pedagogy he sought to popularize in the United States. Neef shared Pestalozzi's zeal for educational reform, social amelioration, natural education, sense experience, and child permissiveness. In contrast to his Swiss mentor, Neef was always a rationalist and never a romantic, always a republican and never a benevolent paternalist. Pestalozzi was always the European, but Neef, who proudly considered himself a frontier backwoodsman, became an American. It was as a rationalist, a frontiersman, a republican, and an American that he sought to naturalize Pestalozzi's educational method.

Neef As a Comparative Educator   While William Maclure certainly deserves serious study as a comparative educator, it would be an exaggeration to attempt to depict Neef as a comparative educator in the strict sense of the term. However, he was not unlike the twentieth century educator who attempts to use his expertise to aid the educational development of an emerging nation. When Neef came to the United States in 1806, he arrived in an underdeveloped nation. Formal educational institutions were primitive; instructional methods were either archaic or rudimentary; economic support for schools was slight or nonexistent. As Monroe and others have indicated, Neef may have been too far ahead of formal educational development. The common-school movement was not even a vague proposal. Although he established his various schools in Pennsylvania, Kentucky, and Indiana, these institutions failed to create any lasting impression on American educators.

When considered in terms of the broader aspects of educational history and theory, the efforts of Neef and Maclure give strong evidence of the transmission of European ideas, theories, and practices to the United States. Neef was trained directly by Pestalozzi in Switzerland, taught in Paris, came to Philadelphia, and then migrated westward to the Indiana-Kentucky frontier. Maclure came from England to the United States, became a citizen, returned to Europe where he visited Pestalozzi, Fellenberg, and Owen, tried to establish an agricultural school in Spain, sought to popularize Pestalozzianism in the United States, and died in Mexico still contemplating further educational experimentation. It would be no exaggeration to refer to both Neef and Maclure as international educators, as schoolmen of the Atlantic community. In fact, their efforts anticipated much of the later interchange of persons and ideas that occurred in the later nineteenth and twentieth centuries.

Neef as a Social Theorist   Neither Neef, Maclure, nor Owen were myopic about the relationship of the school to society.

They did not entertain a narrow, restricted, or closed view of the school. Their conception of the school as a societal agent anticipated many of the ideas developed by later educators and social theorists. The brief experiment of Owen and Maclure at New Harmony, in which Neef participated, was a bold attempt to use the school as an agency of social reconstruction.

Neef recognized that education served the needs and embodied the values of the particular society that it served. Although he never lost sight of the commonalities embedded in human nature, Neef believed that American education ought to be responsive to the particular demands and requirements of the political, social, and economic realities of the United States. He never hesitated to refer to republican ideals and to the means that were needed to perpetuate and sustain these ideals.

Neef and Maclure recognized that social and industrial change had cultural and educational ramifications. They felt that formal educational theory and practice had ignored major social changes and had grown increasingly irrelevant to the requirements induced by political and industrial revolution. Both men directed their educational efforts to redirecting the school's content and practice in order to reduce the lag or gap between social realities and formal education. Both Neef and Maclure clearly anticipated Herbert Spencer's question, "What knowledge is of most worth?"

Neef as a Progressive Educator   Several interpreters of Neef's contribution to American educational history have viewed him as a predecessor of the progressive educators such as Francis Parker, William Heard Kilpatrick, and Harold Rugg. Like other educational reformers of the nineteenth century, Neef had much in common with the twentieth century progressives.[8] He emphasized child interests, student self-government, activities, projects, physical exercises, nature studies, permissiveness, field trips, and the scientific method. Neef clearly construed the teacher's function to be that of a guide rather than as a task master. Like the progressives, Neef attacked excessively verbal instruction, exclusive reliance on literature, and emphasis on memorization. Since he was part of the genre of Pestalozzi, Fellenberg, and others, it is not difficult to place him among the ranks of the progressive educators.

Failure or Success?   Was Neef a failure or a success? Did he accomplish his end of popularizing Pestalozzian education? Such a direct question cannot be answered either simply or satisfactorily. Most interpreters, including this writer, agree that Neef's attempt to popularize Pestalozzianism had little impact on the course of American institutional development. Lockwood, Monroe, Bayles and Hood, and other historians agree that Neef's work was rather isolated. Most concur that Henry Barnard's *American Journal of Education*, 1856–1881, and his *Pestalozzi and Pestalozzianism*, 1862, were sources more sustained and pervasive in popularizing Pestalozzi's educational theory than Neef's *Sketch* and other writings.[9] Although educational historians agree that Edward A. Sheldon's Oswego movement was a pale and formalized version of Pestalozzianism, they recognize it as having a major impact on American school practice. It was Sheldon's object lesson which came to be known as the Pestalozzian method to thousands of American teachers in the years after the Civil War.[10] According to Bayles and Hood:

... of the approximately 1400 who graduated from Oswego during the first quarter-century of its existence and who went from there to almost every state in the Union, many were those who took with them the "methods" but not the spirit of Pestalozzi.[11]

Although Neef's school at the Falls of the Schuylkill enjoyed a brief success, all of his later schools failed. Neef may have moved so frequently that he was unable to firmly establish his schools in any particular locality. His religious, educational, economic and antislavery opinions were too controversial and unpopular with many of his contemporaries. Like Pestalozzi, he seemed to be inept as an educational administrator; unlike Pestalozzi, Neef failed to devote sufficient attention to teacher preparation. Although Pestalozzi had many disciples, Neef had no significant followers.

Robert Owen's New Harmony failed as a communitarian experiment, and Maclure's school system failed with it. As a director of the community's largest school, Neef's work at New Harmony also failed. Perhaps, the association of Neef's Pestalozzianism with Owenite socialism may have seriously injured the attempt to popularize the method of education.

It may have been historically indiscreet to reply to the question of Neef's success or failure. A conclusion may be more appropriate: Joseph Neef was committed to the ideal of Pestalozzian education, and he struggled to achieve the ideal. As is the case of most men who are so committed, he changed the ideal by his own hand; like all men, he never completely realized his goal.

NOTES

Chapter 1

1. Published materials dealing with Neef such as C. D. Gardette, "Pestalozzi in America," *The Galaxy*, IV (August, 1867), 432–439; Will S. Monroe, *History of the Pestalozzian Movement in the United States* (Syracuse: C. W. Bardeen, 1907); Will S. Monroe, "Joseph Neef and Pestalozzianism in America," *Education*, XIV (April, 1894), 449–461; Theodore Schreiber, "First Pestalozzian in the New World," *The German-American Review*, IV (October, 1942), 25–27; C. H. Wood, "The First Disciple of Pestalozzi in America," *Indiana School Journal*, XXXVII (Nov., 1892), 559–665, depict him as a Pestalozzi disciple who first introduced that method in the United States. The following unpublished dissertations—Thomas A. Barlow, "Channels of Pestalozzianism into the United States," University of Kansas, 1963; Helen Elliott, "Development of the New Harmony Community with Special Reference to Education," Indiana University, 1933; Robert L. Phillips, "Joseph Neef and His Methods of Teaching," Eastern Illinois University, 1962—also emphasize the similarities in the educational theory and practice of Neef and Pestalozzi.
2. R. G. Burton, *Napoleon's Campaigns in Italy* (London: George Allen and Unwin Ltd., 1931), p. 4.
3. Ibid., pp. 4–5.
4. Workingmen's Institute and Library MS, Caroline Dale Snedeker, "My Alsatian Grandfather" (December, 1905), pp. 3–4. An unpublished typescript.
5. Illinois Historical Survey MS. J.N. 1.2 1/2. Army of the Rhine, 5th Division, 2nd Brigade. Certificate that Francis Joseph Neef had

served honorably. Dated 5 ventose, an 9. (February 24, 1801), microfilm.

6. Kate Silber, *Pestalozzi: The Man and His Work* (London: Routledge and Kegan Paul, 1960), p. 46.

7. Carline Dale Snedeker, *The Town of the Fearless* (Garden City, N.Y.: Doubleday, Doran, and Co., 1931), p. 57.

8. Silber, *Pestalozzi*, p. 34.

9. Roger de Guimps, *Pestalozzi: His Aim and Work* (Syracuse: C. W. Bardeen, 1889), pp. 99–100.

10. "Report of the Commission of Schools at Burgdorf," Ibid., pp. 101–102.

11. Joseph Neef, *Sketch of a Plan and Method of Education* (Philadelphia: privated printed, 1808), p. 2.

12. Silber, *Pestalozzi*, p. 123.

13. Hermann Krusi, *Pestalozzi: His Life, Work, and Influence* (Cincinnati: Van Antwerp, Bragg, and Co., 1875), p. 93.

14. Neef, *Sketch of a Plan and Method of Education*, p. 2.

15. Silber, *Pestalozzi*, pp. 130–131.

16. Illinois Historical Survey MS. J.N. 1.7. William Maclure, Rome. To Joseph Neef, Falls of the Schulkill (sic), Pennsylvania, 3pp. (February 10, 1812), microfilm.

17. Ramsauer's account as cited in de Guimps, p. 123.

18. Monroe, "Joseph Neef," 455; also Snedeker, *Town of the Fearless*, p. 66.

19. Johann Heinrich Pestalozzi, *The Method, A Report by Pestalozzi*, in the appendix of *How Gertrude Teaches Her Children* (Syracuse: C. W. Bardeen, 1900), pp. 199–211.

20. Ibid., p. 200.

21. Ibid., p. 202.

22. Pestalozzi, *How Gertrude Teaches Her Children*, p. 23.

23. Monroe, "Neef," 450; Snedeker, *Town of the Fearless*, pp. 63–64.

24. Illinois Historical Survey MS. J.N. 1.3. Joseph Neef, Paris. To Heinrich Pestalozzi, Yverdon, Switzerland, 1p. (ca. 1803–04), microfilm.

Chapter 2

1. Arthur E. Bestor, Jr., *Backwoods Utopias* (Philadelphia: University of Pennsylvania Press, 1950), p. 146.

2. W. H. G. Armytage, *Heavens Below: Utopian Experiments in England, 1560–1960* (London: Routledge and Kegan Paul, 1961), p. 118.

3. For short biographical sketches of Maclure, see Samuel G. Morton, *A Memoir of William Maclure* (Philadelphia: T. K. and P. G. Collins, 1841); and J. Percy Moore, "William Maclure—Scientist and Humanitarian," *Proceedings of the American Philosophical Society*, 91, No. 3, (August, 1947). William Maclure was a man of many interests. In addition to his educational and philanthropic efforts, he was interested in the study of geology and made some of the first geological surveys of the United States. On July 20, 1809, he read a paper on the geology of the United States at a meeting of the American Philosophical Society. He later wrote *Observations on the Geology of the United States of America, 1818.*

4. Monroe, *Pestalozzian Movement*, pp. 43–44.

5. Bestor, *Backwoods Utopias*, p. 148.

6. William Maclure to Marie D. Fretageot, May 22, 1820, in Arthur E. Bestor, Jr., ed., *Education and Reform at New Harmony: Correspondence of William Maclure and Marie Duclos Fretageot, 1820–1833* (Indianapolis: Indiana Historical Society Publication, 1948), p. 301.

7. Monroe, *Pestalozzian Movement*, p. 44.

8. Neef, *Sketch*, p. 5.

9. Illinois Historical Survey MS. J.N. 1.1 William Maclure, Paris, Agreement with Joseph Neef, 2 pp. (March 19, 1806) microfilm. 3,200 Livres Tournois was equivalent to approximately six hundred dollars.

10. Illinois Historical Survey MS. J.N. 1.6 J. Cox Barnet, Commercial Agent of the United States. Certificate recommending Joseph Neef to protection of American officers and citizens in traveling to America. Paris, 2 pp. (March 20, 1806), microfilm.

11. Monroe, *Pestalozzian Movement*, pp. 77–78. Christopher Dock was a Mennonite schoolmaster who wrote his treatise in German about the middle of the eighteenth century. It was later published by Christopher Sauer in 1770.

12. H. G. Good, *A History of American Education* (New York: The Macmillan Co., 1962), p. 172.

13. Neef, *Sketch*, pp. 165–166.

14. Etienne Bonnot de Condillac, *Logic of Condillac, Translated by Joseph Neef, as an Illustration of the Plan of Education Established at His School Near Philadelphia* (Philadelphia: Printed for the Author, 1809).

15. Joseph Neef, *The Method of Instructing Children Rationally, in*

the *Arts of Writing and Reading* (Philadelphia: Printed for the Author, 1813).

16. Gardette, "Pestalozzi in America," 436–437.

17. Workingmen's Institute and Library, New Harmony, Indiana MS, A Catalogue of the Students formerly at the Academy at the Falls of the Schuylkill. Addressed to Samuel Eden of New Orleans, Mr. Owen's Agent. Although this document is undated, it was probably sent to Eden during the period from 1825 to 1827.

18. Gardette, "Pestalozzi in America," 437. Two brothers named Gardette attended the school: Joseph Gardette, who later became a dentist, and E. G. Gardette, who continued to correspond with Neef's son, Victor, after the school had closed. Although C. D. Gardette, the author of the *Galaxy* article, did not specify which brother provided the information used, it was probably E. B. Gardette.

19. Ibid.

20. Ibid.

21. Ibid.

22. Neef, *Sketch*, p. 7.

23. Gardette, "Pestalozzi in America," 437–438. Neef disliked wearing a hat since the slightest pressure on his head would cause a headache. Neef was a very informal person who did not adhere to the usual conventions of the time.

24. For a biography of Farragut see Charles Lee Lewis, *David Glasgow Farragut: Admiral in the Making* (Annapolis: United States Naval Academy, 1941). Farragut, who first saw service in the War of 1812, was later recognized as an expert on naval ordnance. He commanded the *Saratoga* during the Mexican War, and won distinction during the Civil War.

25. Lewis, *Farragut*, p. 111.

26. Ibid.

27. Neef, *Sketch*, p. 75.

28. Illinois Historical Survey MS. J.N. 1.9. William Maclure, Paris, to Joseph Neef, Philadelphia. 4pp. (February 4, 1815), microfilm.

29. William Maclure, *Opinions on Various Subjects, Dedicated to the Industrious Producers.* I, (New Harmony: School Press, 1831), p. 3; see also Vol. II, pp. 30–32.

30. Neef, *Sketch*, p. 167.

31. Illinois Historical Survey MS. J.N. 1.9. William Maclure, Paris, to Joseph Neef, Philadelphia, 4 pp. (February 4, 1815), microfilm.

32. Gardette, "Pestalozzi in America," 438–439.
33. Illinois Historical Survey MS. J.N. 1. 11. William Maclure, Philadelphia, to Joseph Neef, Louisville, Kentucky, 1 p. (May 23, 1816), microfilm.
34. Ibid.

Chapter 3

1. A number of books have appeared on Owen's New Harmony community. One of the earliest was George B. Lockwood, *The New Harmony Movement* (New York: D. Appleton and Co., 1905). Although more sources have come to light since Lockwood's book was written, it is still useful. Chapter XX, "The Educational Experiment," pp. 209–293, is of particular interest to educational historians. Richard W. Leopold, *Robert Dale Owen: A Biography* (Cambridge: Harvard University Press, 1940), contains a clearly written section on New Harmony, pp. 24–46, which neatly organizes the many confusing issues and episodes relating to the community's brief history as the center of Owen's experiment.

Bestor's *Backwoods Utopias* is a scholarly and well-documented treatment. While devoted primarily to analyzing the communitarian aspects of Owen's experiment, Bestor's Chapter VI, "Educational Allies of Communitarianism," is an excellent discussion of the theoretical bases of New Harmony's schools. Bestor's *Education and Reform at New Harmony* is a careful editing of William Maclure's and Marie Duclos Fretageot's letters.

William E. Wilson, *The Angel and the Serpent* (Bloomington: Indiana University Press, 1964), deals with both the Rappite and Owenite communities. Marguerite Young, *Angel in the Forest* (New York: Charles Scribner's Sons, 1945), is interesting as a psychological and somewhat poetical treatment but not of much assistance to the historian. Paul Brown, *Twelve Months in New Harmony* (Cincinnati: William Hill Woodward, 1827), was written by a participant in the community. Although his caustic criticism of Owen weakens the account, Brown's close friendship with Neef makes it a useful work. Robert Dale Owen, *Threading My Way: Twenty-seven Years of Autobiography* (New York: G. W. Carleton and Co., 1874), contains an account of New Harmony and commentaries on some of the participants. Snedeker's *Town of the Fearless*, an historical novel about New Harmony, was written by the granddaughter of Robert Owen and Joseph Neef.

2. Bestor, *Backwoods Utopias*, pp. 133–134.
3. For treatments of Owen, see G. D. H. Cole, *Robert Owen* (Boston: Little, Brown and Co., 1925); Rowland Hill Harvey, *Robert Owen: Social Idealist* (Berkeley: University of California Press, 1949); Robert Owen, *The Life of Robert Owen, by Himself* (New York: Alfred Knopf, 1920). For the Rappites, see John S. Duss, *George Rapp and his Associates* (Indianapolis: The Hollenbeck Press, 1914); Wilson, *Angel and the Serpent*, Part I, pp. 5–92, provides a clearly written treatment of the Rappite community of Harmonie which preceded the Owenite community.
4. For accounts of Owen's first trip to the United States, see Donald Macdonald, *The Diaries of Donald Macdonald, 1824–1826* (Indianapolis: Indiana Historical Society Publications, 1942); and William Owen, *Diary of William Owen from November 10, 1824, to April 20, 1825*, Joel H. Hiatt, ed., (Indianapolis: Indiana Historical Society Publications, 1906).
5. Bestor, *Backwoods Utopias*, pp. 157–158.
6. Ibid., p. viii.
7. Ibid., p. 3.
8. For a discussion of Pestalozzi's world view, see Gerald L. Gutek, *Pestalozzi and Education* (New York: Random House, 1968), pp. 52–79.
9. Bestor, *Backwoods Utopias*, pp. 134–135.
10. George S. Counts, *Dare the School Build a New Social Order?* (New York: The John Day Co., 1932).
11. Theodore Brameld, *Toward a Reconstructed Philosophy of Education* (New York: Holt, Rinehart and Winston, 1956), p. 151.
12. For an extensive treatment of progressive education, see, Lawrence A. Cremin, *The Transformation of the School: Progressivism in American Education, 1876–1957* (New York: Alfred A. Knopf and Random House, Inc., 1961); C. A. Bowers, *The Progressive Educator and the Depression: The Radical Years* (New York: Random House, 1969), discusses the transition of certain progressive educators into advocates of social reconstruction.
13. Merle Curti, *The Social Ideas of American Educators* (Paterson, New Jersey: Littlefield, Adams, and Co., 1959), p. 154. Curti's book contains interpretations of both Mann and Barnard as social reformers, pp. 101–168.
14. W. T. Harris, "Introduction," in Lockwood, p. xi.
15. Lockwood, p. 84.
16. Ibid., pp. 105–108.

17. Illinois Historical Survey, Urbana, Illinois MS. JN. 1.15. William Maclure, Philadelphia, to Joseph Neef, Floydsburg, Kentucky, 2pp. (October 28, 1825), microfilm.
18. For accounts of the Philanthropist's voyage, see Bestor, *Backwoods Utopia,* pp. 158–159; Wilson, *Angel and the Serpent,* pp. 136–143.
19. For a biography of Say, see Harry B. Weiss and Grace M. Ziegler, *Thomas Say: Early American Naturalist* (Springfield, Illinois: Charles C. Thomas Publisher, 1931).
20. Ibid., pp. 170–171.
21. Ibid., pp. 167–169.
22. Richard W. Leopold's *Robert Dale Owen: A Biography* (Cambridge: Harvard University Press, 1940), is an excellent treatment of Owen's life. For a discussion of Owen's own system of education, see Robert Dale Owen, *An Outline of the System of Education at New Lanark* (Cincinnati: Deming and Wood, 1825).
23. Owen, *Threading My Way,* p. 283.
24. Illinois Historical Survey, Urbana, Illinois MS. J.N. 1. 16. William Maclure, New Harmony, to Joseph Neef, Louisville, 1 p. (February 20, 1826), microfilm.

Chapter 4

1. William Maclure in *American Journal of Science and Arts,* X (1826), as cited in Lockwood, *New Harmony* p. 236.
2. Elliott, "Development of the New Harmony Community," p. 78.
3. Lockwood, *New Harmony,* pp. 236–238.
4. Ibid., p. 243; Elliott, "Development of the New Harmony Community," pp. 74–75.
5. Brown, *Twelve Months,* p. 115. Neef was a friend of Paul Brown who was a caustic critic of Robert Owen. Brown's book contains several sections which describe Neef's work at New Harmony and his opposition to Owen.
6. Ibid., pp. 112–113.
7. Victor Colin Duclos, "Diary and Recollections," in *Indiana as Seen by Early Travelers,* Harlow Lindley, ed., (Indianapolis: Indiana Historical Collections, 1916), p. 546.
8. Karl Bernhard, *Travels Through North America, During the Years 1825 and 1826* (Philadelphia: Carey, Lea & Carey, 1828), in Lindley, pp. 435–436.
9. Ibid., pp. 424–425.
10. Ibid., p. 429.

11. Owen, *Threading My Way*, pp. 283–284.
12. Lockwood, *New Harmony*, p. 260.
13. For accounts of the formation of the separate societies, see Bestor, *Backwoods Utopias*, pp. 184–185; Wilson, *Angel and the Serpent*, p. 177.
14. Brown, *Twelve Months*, p. 114.
15. Bestor, *Correspondence*, p. 375.
16. Elliott, "Development of the New Harmony Community," p. 78.
17. Madame Fretageot to William Maclure, New Harmony, August 11, 1826, in Bestor, *Correspondence*, p. 352.
18. William Maclure to Madame Fretageot, Cincinnati, August 29, 1826, ibid., p. 362.
19. William Maclure to Madame Fretageot, Louisville, September 19, 1826, ibid., p. 368.
20. Madame Fretageot to William Maclure, New Harmony, March 2, 1827, ibid., pp. 289–290.
21. Lockwood, *New Harmony*, p. 246.
22. Brown, *Twelve Months*, pp. 94–95.
23. For discussions of confusing Owen-Maclure financial controversy, see Bestor, *Backwoods Utopias*, pp. 197–199; Bestor, *Correspondence*, pp. 334–335, 392–393; Wilson, *Angel and the Serpent*, p. 179.
24. Bestor, *Backwoods Utopias*, pp. 192–193.
25. Lockwood, *New Harmony*, pp. 252–253.
26. Leopold, *Owen*, pp. 42–43.
27. Brown, *Twelve Months*, p. 80.
28. Ibid., p. 107.
29. Ibid.
30. Ibid.
31. Ibid., p. 108.
32. Lockwood, *New Harmony*, pp. 286–287.
33. Ibid., p. 291.

Chapter 5

1. Illinois Historical Survey, MS. J.N. 1.18. Benjamin Tappan, Steubenville, Ohio, to Joseph Neef, Cincinnati. 1 p. (July 12, 1827), microfilm.
2. Monroe, "Joseph Neef," p. 454.
3. Workingmen's Institute, New Harmony, Card File of Local History.
4. Snedeker, *Town of the Fearless*, pp. 310–311.

5. For a discussion of Owen's descendants and New Harmony after Robert Owen's experiment, see Lockwood, *New Harmony*, pp. 314–377. Wilson, *Angel and the Serpent*, pp. 183–213. Bestor, *Backwoods Utopias*, pp. 202–229, treats the aftermath of Owen's experiment in the context of communitarianism.

6. Workingmen's Institute, New Harmony, Indiana, MS, by Caroline Dale Snedeker, "My Alsatian Grandfather" (December, 1905), pp. 27–28. Unpublished typescript.

7. Ibid.

Chapter 6

1. Johann Amos Comenius, 1592–1670, had developed an educational method based on sense realism and the recognition of childhood as a natural stage of human growth. His books include the *Encyclopaedia of all the Sciences*, 1630; *Janua linquarum reserata*, or the *Gate of Languages Unlocked*, 1631; *Orbis sensualium pictus*, 1658, an illustrated textbook for teaching Latin. Comenius' most significant pedagogical work, the *Great Didactic*, 1657, attempted to provide a method for teaching every subject. English translations of Comenius' works are: M. W. Keatinge's *The Great Didactic of John Amos Comenius* (London: Adam and Charles Black, 1896); Vladimir Jelinek's *The Analytical Didactic of Comenius* (Chicago: University of Chicago Press, 1953); *The Orbis Pictus of John Amos Comenius* (Syracuse: C. W. Bardeen, 1887).

   Jean Jacques Rousseau, 1712–1778, advocated a permissive, naturalistic method of education in *Emile*, 1762. Among English translations are: *Emile*, translated by Barbara Foxley (London: J. M. Dent and Sons, 1911); *The Emile of Jean Jacques Rousseau: Selections*, translated and edited by William Boyd (New York: Bureau of Publications, Teachers College, Columbia University, 1962).

2. For a discussion of the concept of child depravity, see Sanford Fleming, *Children and Puritanism: The Place of Children in the Life and Thought of the New England Churches, 1620–1847* (New Haven: Yale University Press, 1933).

3. William J. McGucken, S. J., *The Catholic Way in Education* (Chicago: Loyola University Press, 1962), pp. 22–26.

4. *How Gertrude Teaches Her Children*, pp. 18–19.

5. *Logic of Condillac*, pp. 74–75. Etienne Bonnot de Condillac,

1715–1780, was a French sensationalist philosopher who reduced all mental processes to sensory operations. Outside of
Neef's pioneer translation, English translations of Condillac's
work are scarce. An exception is *Condillac's Treatise on the Sensations*, translated by Geraldine Carr. (Los Angeles: University
of Southern California Press, 1930).

6. Paul Monroe, *A Brief Course in the History of Education* (New
   York: The Macmillan Co., 1934), p. 301. First published in 1907.
7. Johann Heinrich Pestalozzi, *Leonard and Gertrude*, in Henry
   Barnard, ed., *Pestalozzi and Pestalozzianism* (New York: Brownell Publisher, 1862), pp. 592–593.
8. For Maclure's socioeconomic and educational theories, see Maclure, *Opinions*.
9. *Logic of Condillac*, p. 9.
10. Pestalozzi, *How Gertrude Teaches Her Children*, p. 28.
11. Joseph Neef, *Sketch*, p. 17.
12. For a clearly written description of progressive education, see
    Meyer, *The Development of Education in the Twentieth Century*,
    pp. 64–107.
13. Neef, *Sketch*, p. 98.
14. Ibid., p. 27.
15. Ibid., p. 165.

Chapter 7

1. John Locke, *An Essay Concerning Human Understanding*, Ray-
   mond Wilburn, ed. (New York: E. P. Dutton and Co., 1947).
2. Isaiah Berlin, *The Age of Enlightenment: The Eighteenth Century
   Philosophers* (Boston: Houghton Mifflin Co., 1956), pp. 266–268.
3. *Logic of Condillac*, p. 1.
4. Illinois Historical Survey MS. J.N. 1.13. William Maclure, Philadelphia, to Joseph Neef, Louisville, 4pp. (February 1, 1817),
   microfilm.
5. *Logic of Condillac*, pp. 26–27.
6. Ibid., p. 15.
7. Ibid., pp. 14–15.
8. S. J. Curtis and M. E. A. Boultwood, *A Short History of Educational
   Ideas* (London: University Tutorial Press, Ltd., 1965), pp. 340–
   341.
9. Gutek, *Pestalozzi and Education*, p. 89.
10. Ibid., pp. 92–93.

11. Neef, *Sketch*, p. 63.
12. Ibid., p. 12.
13. Ibid., p. 13.
14. Pestalozzi, *How Gertrude Teaches Her Children*, p. 115.
15. Neef, *Sketch*, p. 14.

Chapter 8

1. Neef, *Sketch*, p. 85.
2. Gutek, *Pestalozzi and Education*, pp. 107–110.
3. For an example of the formalized English object lesson see Elizabeth Mayo, *Lessons on Objects, As Given to Children, Between the Ages of Six and Eight, in a Pestalozzian School* (London: Seeley and Burnside, 1835); for the Oswego method of object teaching see E. A. Sheldon, *Lessons on Objects, Graduated Series* (New York: Charles Scribner's, 1863); the history of the Oswego movement was written by Ned H. Dearborn, *The Oswego Movement in American Education* (New York: Teachers College, Columbia University, 1925).
4. Neef, *Sketch*, p. 8.
5. Ibid., pp. 8–11.
6. Ibid., p. 9.
7. Ibid., p. 121.
8. Ibid., pp. 6–7.
9. *Gertrude Teaches Her Children*, p. 79.
10. *Logic of Condillac*, p. 23.

Chapter 9

1. Pestalozzi, *How Gertrude Teaches Her Children*, p. 87.
2. From Jacob Willetts, *The Scholar's Arithmetic* (Poughkeepsie, 1817), as cited in Clifton Johnson, *Old-Time Schools and School-Books* (New York: Dover Publications, 1963), p. 310.
3. Neef, *Sketch*, p. 16.
4. Sister Mary Romana Walch, *Pestalozzi and the Pestalozzian Theory of Education: A Critical Study* (Washington: The Catholic University Press, 1952), p. 135.
5. Pestalozzi, *How Gertrude Teaches Her Children*, p. 117.
6. Walch, *Pestalozzi*, p. 134.
7. Neef, *Method*, p. 1.
8. Neef, *Sketch*, p. 43.

9. Ibid., p. 53.

10. Pestalozzi, *How Gertrude Teaches Her Children*, pp. 124–125.

11. Pestalozzi, "The Method of Instruction," in Barnard, p. 697.

12. Neef, *Sketch*, p. 48.

13. Neef, *Method*, p. 88.

14. Neef, *Sketch*, p. 7.

15. *Logic of Condillac*, p. 79.

16. Ibid., p. 84.

17. Pestalozzi, *How Gertrude Teaches Her Children*, p. 150.

18. Ibid., p. 90.

19. Neef, *Sketch*, pp. 78–79.

20. For a discussion of Noah Webster's educational ideas see Henry Steele Commager, "Schoolmaster to America," which is the introductory essay to the reprinted edition of *Noah Webster's American Spelling Book* (New York: Bureau of Publications, Teachers College, Columbia University, 1962). Webster's *American Spelling Book* was first published in 1831.

21. Neef, *Sketch*, pp. 55–56.

22. Ibid., p. 54.

23. Ibid., p. 111.

24. Ibid., pp. 112–114.

25. Lockwood, *New Harmony*, p. 289.

26. For a discussion of Herbert Spencer see *Herbert Spencer on Education*, Andreas Kazamias, ed., (New York: Bureau of Publications, Teachers College, Columbia University, 1966).

27. For a discussion of the arguments against classical languages, see Edward A. Krug, *The Shaping of the American High School* (New York: Harper and Row Publishers, 1964), pp. 32–34, 84–85, 278–280, 308–309, 324–325, 337–338.

28. Neef, *Sketch*, p. 87.

29. Ibid., p. 89.

30. William H. Kilpatrick, "The Project Method," *Teachers College Record*, XIX (September, 1918), 319–335.

31. Neef, *Sketch*, p. 90.

32. Walch, *Pestalozzi*, p. 126.

33. For a discussion of early nineteenth century geography texts, see Johnson, *Old-Time Schools and School-Books*, pp. 318–362.

34. From Nathaniel Dwight, *Dwight's Geography*, 1795, as cited in Johnson, p. 340.

35. For a discussion of *Adam's Geography*, 1818, see Johnson, *Old-Time Schools and School-Books*, p. 348.

36. Neef, *Sketch,* pp. 147–148.
37. Ibid., pp. 148–149.
38. Walch, *Pestalozzi,* pp. 128–129.
39. Silber, *Pestalozzi,* p. 146.
40. Illinois Historical Survey, MS. J.N. 1.9., Letter of William Maclure, Paris, to Joseph Neef, Philadelphia, 4pp. (February 4, 1815) microfilm.
41. Neef, *Sketch,* p. 106.
42. Ibid., p. 107.
43. Ibid., p. 108.
44. Ibid., pp. 108–109.

Chapter 10

1. For example, see Charles W. Hackensmith, *Biography of Joseph Neef, Educator in the Ohio Valley, 1809–1854* (New York: Carlton Press, 1973).
2. Pestalozzi, *How Gertrude Teaches Her Children,* p. 183.
3. Neef, *Sketch,* p. 23.
4. Rousseau, *Emile,* p. 38.
5. Neef, *Sketch,* pp. 83–84.
6. Ibid., p. 80.
7. Ibid., pp. 75–76.
8. Ibid., pp. 76–77.
9. Ibid., p. 78.
10. Ibid., p. 79.
11. Pestalozzi, *How Gertrude Teaches,* pp. 182–183.
12. Silber, *Pestalozzi,* p. 149.
13. Pestalozzi, *How Gertrude Teaches,* p. 185.
14. Neef, *Sketch,* p. 75.
15. Ibid.
16. Johnson, *Old-Time Schools and School-Books,* pp. 96–97.
17. *The New-England Primer,* intro. by Paul Ford (New York: Teachers College, Columbia University, 1962), pp. 88–90. (Reprinted from the 1897 edition published by Dodd, Mead, and Co.)
18. Pestalozzi, *Leonard and Gertrude,* p. 660.
19. Neef, *Sketch,* p. 76.
20. Silber, *Pestalozzi,* p. 64.
21. Pestalozzi, *Leonard and Gertrude,* p. 551.
22. For Maclure's socioeconomic and educational views, see Maclure, *Opinions.*

23. Neef, *Sketch*, p. 28.
24. Ibid., p. 29.
25. Ibid., p. 82.
26. Ibid.
27. Pestalozzi, *Christopher and Elizabeth*, in Barnard, p. 667.
28. Neef, *Sketch*, p. 27.

Chapter 11

1. Monroe, *Pestalozzian Movement*, pp. 77–78.
2. Ibid., pp. 123–126.
3. Newton Edwards and Herman G. Richey, *The School in the American Social Order* (Boston: Houghton Mifflin Co., 1963), p. 581.
4. William M. French, *America's Educational Tradition* (Boston: D. C. Heath and Co., 1964), p. 131.
5. Meyer, *Educational History*, p. 234.
6. Lockwood, *New Harmony*, pp. 209–293.
7. Bestor, *Backwoods Utopias*, pp. 133–159.
8. Emma L. Farrell, "New Harmony Experiment," *Peabody Journal of Education* (May, 1938), pp. 357–361.
9. Barnard, *Pestalozzi and Pestalozzianism*.
10. For a series of lesson plans based on object teaching, see E. A. Sheldon, *Lessons on Objects* (New York: Charles Scribner's Sons, 1863).
11. Ernest E. Bayles and Bruce L. Hood, *Growth of American Educational Thought and Practice* (New York: Harper and Row Publishers, 1966), p. 142.

BIBLIOGRAPHY

Primary Sources

Manuscripts

Manuscript Collection in the Illinois Historical Survey of the University of Illinois, Urbana, Illinois: Joseph Neef Papers, 1799–1849, microfilm, 22 items.

Manuscript Collection in the Workingmen's Institute, New Harmony, Indiana: Maclure-Fretageot Correspondence; Papers of William Maclure, Joseph Neef, and others associated with Robert Owen's New Harmony experiment; typescripts by Caroline Dale Snedeker and Caroline C. Pelham.

Books

Bestor, Arthur E., Jr., ed., *Education and Reform at New Harmony: Correspondence of William Maclure and Marie Duclos Fretageot, 1820–1833*. Indianapolis: Indiana Historical Society, 1948.

Brown, Paul, *Twelve Months in New Harmony; Representing a Faithful Account of the Principal Occurrences Which Have Taken Place There Within That Period; Interspersed with Remarks*. Cincinnati: Wm. Woodward, 1827.

Condillac, Etienne Bonnot de. *Logic of Condillac, Translated by Joseph Neef, As an Illustration of the Plan of Education Established at His School Near Philadelphia*. Philadelphia: Printed for the Author, 1809.

Maclure, William. *Opinions on Various Subjects, Dedicated to the*

Industrious Producers. New Harmony: Printed at the School Press, Vol. 1, 1831; Vol., II, 1837; Vol. III, 1838.

Macdonald, Donald. *The Diaries of Donald Macdonald, 1824–1826*. Indianapolis: Indiana Historical Society, 1942.

Neef, Joseph. *The Method of Instructing Children Rationally in the Arts of Writing and Reading*. Philadelphia: Printed for the Author, 1813.

Neef, Joseph. *Sketch of a Plan and Method of Education, Founded on an Analysis of the Human Faculties, and Natural Reason, Suitable for the Offspring of a Free People, and for all Rational Beings*. Philadelphia: Printed for the Author, 1808.

Owen, Robert Dale. *An Outline of the System of Education at New Lanark*. Cincinnati: Deming and Wood, 1825.

Owen, William. *Diary of William Owen from November 10, 1824 to April 20, 1825*. Indianapolis: Indiana Historical Society, 1906.

Pears, Thomas Clinton, Jr., ed., *New Harmony: An Adventure in Happiness: Papers of Thomas and Sarah Pears*. Indianapolis: Indiana Historical Society, 1933.

Secondary Sources

Books

Armytage, W. H. G. *Heavens Below: Utopian Experiments in England, 1560–1960*. London: Routledge and Kegan Paul, 1961.

Barnard, Henry, ed., *Pestalozzi and Pestalozzianism*. New York: F. C. Brownell Co., 1862.

Bayles, Ernest E. and Hood, Bruce L. *Growth of American Educational Thought and Practice*. New York: Harper and Row, Publishers, 1966.

Berlin, Isaiah. *The Age of the Enlightenment*. Boston: Houghton Mifflin Co., 1956.

Best, John H., ed. *Benjamin Franklin on Education*. New York: Bureau of Publications, Teachers College, Columbia University, 1962.

Bestor, Arthur E., Jr. *Backwoods Utopias: The Sectarian and Owenite Phases of Communitarian Socialism in America, 1663–1829*. Philadelphia: University of Pennsylvania Press, 1950.

Bowers, C. A. *The Progressive Educator and the Depression: The Radical Years*. New York: Random House, 1969.

Boyd, William, ed. *The Emile of Jean Jacques Rousseau: Selections*.

New York: Teachers College Press, Teachers College, Columbia University, 1962.

Burton, R. G. *Napoleon's Campaigns in Italy*. London: George Allen and Unwin Ltd., 1931.

Butts, R. Freeman and Cremin, Lawrence A. *A History of Education in American Culture*. New York: Henry Holt and Co., 1953.

Condillac, Etienne Bonnot de. *Condillac's Treatise on the Sensations*. tr. Geraldine Carr. Los Angeles: University of Southern California, 1930.

Cremin, Lawrence A. *The Transformation of the School: Progressivism in American Education, 1876–1957*. New York: Alfred A. Knopf, Inc. and Random House, Inc., 1961.

Curti, Merle. *The Social Ideas of American Educators*. Peterson, New Jersey: Littlefield, Adams, and Co., 1959.

Curtis, S. J. and Boultwood, M. E. A. *A Short History of Educational Ideas*. London: University Tutorial Press, 1965.

De Guimps, Roger. *Pestalozzi: His Aim and Work*. Syracuse: C. W. Bardeen, 1889.

Edwards, Newton and Richey, Herman G. *The School in the American Social Order*. Boston: Houghton Mifflin Co., 1963.

Ford, Paul L., ed. *The New England Primer*. New York: Teachers College Press, Teachers College, Columbia University, 1962.

French, William M. *America's Educational Tradition*. Boston: D. C. Heath and Co., 1964.

Gutek, Gerald L. *Pestalozzi and Education*. New York: Random House, 1968.

Heafford, Michael. *Pestalozzi: His Thought and Its Relevance Today*. London: Methuen and Co., 1967.

Johnson, Clifton. *Old-Time Schools and School-Books*. New York: Dover Publications, Inc., 1963.

Krusi, Hermann. *Pestalozzi: His Life, Work and Influence*. Cincinnati: Van Antwerp, Bragg, and Co., 1875.

Leopold, Richard W. *Robert Dale Owen*. Cambridge, Mass.: Harvard University Press, 1940.

Lewis, Charles Lee. *David Glasgow Farragut: Admiral in the Making*. Annapolis: United States Naval Institute, 1941.

Lindley, Harlow, ed. *Indiana As Seen by Early Travelers: A Collection of Reprints from Books of Travel, Letters and Diaries Prior to 1830*. Indianapolis: Indiana Historical Commission, 1916.

Lockwood, George B. *The New Harmony Movement*. New York: D. Appleton and Co., 1905.

Meyer, Adolphe E. *An Educational History of the American People.* New York: McGraw-Hill Book Co., 1967.

Monroe, Will A. *History of the Pestalozzian Movement in the United States.* Syracuse: C. W. Bardeen Publisher, 1907.

Noah Webster's American Spelling Book. New York: Bureau of Publications, Teachers College, Columbia University, 1962.

Owen, Robert Dale. *Threading My Way: Twenty-seven Years of Autobiography.* New York: G. W. Carleton and Co., 1874.

Pestalozzi, Johann Heinrich. *How Gertrude Teaches Her Children.* Lucy Holland and Francis Turner, trs. Syracuse: C. W. Bardeen Co., 1907.

Potter, Robert E. *The Stream of American Education.* New York: American Book Co., 1967.

Sampson, R. V. *Progress in the Age of Reason.* Cambridge, Mass.: Harvard University Press, 1956.

Sargent, Herbert H. *Napoleon Bonaparte's First Campaign.* Chicago: A. C. McClurg and Co., 1908.

Sheldon, Edward A. *Lessons on Objects.* New York: Charles Scribner's Sons, 1863.

Silber, Kate. *Pestalozzi: The Man and His Work.* London: Routledge and Kegan Paul, 1960.

Snedeker, Caroline Dale. *The Town of the Fearless.* New York: Doubleday, Doran and Co., 1931.

Walch, Sister Mary Romana. *Pestalozzi and the Pestalozzian Theory of Education: A Critical Study.* Washington: Catholic University Press, 1952.

Weiss, Harry B. and Ziegler, Grace M. *Thomas Say: Early American Naturalist.* Springfield, Ill.: Charles C. Thomas Publisher, 1931.

Wilson, William E. *The Angel and the Serpent: The Story of New Harmony.* Bloomington: Indiana University Press, 1964.

Wilson, William E. *The Wabash.* New York: Rinehart and Co., 1940.

Young, Marguerite. *Angel in the Forest: A Fairy Tale of Two Utopias.* New York: Reynal and Hitchcock, 1945.

Articles

Carman, Ada. "Joseph Neef: A Pestalozzian Pioneer," *Popular Science Monthly*, XLV (July, 1894), 373–375.

Gardette, C. D. "Pestalozzi in America," *The Galaxy*, IV (August, 1867), 432–439.

Gutek, Gerald L. "An Examination of Joseph Neef's Theory of Ethical Education," *History of Education Quarterly*, IX (Summer, 1969), 187–201.

Monroe, Will S. "Joseph Neef and Pestalozzianism in America," *Education*, XIV (April, 1894), 449–461.

Schreiber, Theodore, "First Pestalozzian in the New World," *The German-American Review*, IX (October, 1942), 25–27.

Wood, C. H. "The First Disciple of Pestalozzi in America," *Indiana School Journal*, XXXVII (November, 1892), 559–665.

Unpublished Monographs

Barlow, Thomas A. "Channels of Pestalozzianism into the United States." Unpublished Doctoral dissertation. University of Kansas, 1963.

Elliott, Helen. "Development of the New Harmony Community with Special Reference to Education." Unpublished Master of Arts Thesis. Indiana University, 1933.

Phillips, Robert L. "Joseph Neef and His Method of Teaching." Unpublished Master of Science in Education Thesis. Eastern Illinois University, 1962.

INDEX

JOSEPH NEEF: THE AMERICANIZATION
OF PESTALOZZIANISM
was composed in VIP Melior
by Chapman's Phototypesetting, Fullerton, California,
printed by Thomson-Shore, Inc., Dexter, Michigan,
and bound by John H. Dekker & Sons, Grand Rapids, Michigan.
Project Editor: James R. Travis
Production: Paul R. Kennedy
Book design: Anna F. Jacobs